The
Great
Evasion

Books by
WILLIAM APPLEMAN WILLIAMS

American-Russian Relations, 1781–1947
The Shaping of American Diplomacy, 1750–1955
The Tragedy of American Diplomacy
The Contours of American History
The United States, Cuba, and Castro
The Great Evasion
The Roots of the Modern American Empire

The Great Evasion

AN ESSAY ON THE
CONTEMPORARY
RELEVANCE OF
KARL MARX AND ON
THE WISDOM OF
ADMITTING THE
HERETIC INTO THE
DIALOGUE ABOUT
AMERICA'S FUTURE

by

WILLIAM APPLEMAN WILLIAMS

NEW VIEWPOINTS
A Division of Franklin Watts, Inc.
New York / 1974

Library of Congress Catalog Card Number: 74-6572
Standard Book Number: 531-06478-6 (pbk.)

This book is for
my children

▼

Contents

▼

> *B*etter heresy
> of doctrine, than
> heresy of heart.

John Greenleaf Whittier,
Mary Garvin, Stanza 22

*A*merica's *Great Evasion*

*A*s the ancients
Say wisely, have a care o' th' main
  chance,
And look before you ere you leap;
For as you sow, ye are like to reap.

Samuel Butler,
Hudibras, Part II, Canto II

▼

*T*ill their own dreams at
length deceive 'em,
And oft repeating, they
believe 'em.

Matthew Prior,
Alma, Canto III

▼

*A*MERICA'S great evasion lies in its manipulation of Nature to avoid a confrontation with the human condition and with the challenge of building a true community.

As a poet whose perception was not wholly blurred by his underlying approval of this massive deception, Frederick Jackson Turner understood that his countrymen defined Nature as the frontier and viewed the frontier as "a gate of escape from the bondage of the past." This has been true, not only in the obvious sense of conquering and managing (and often wasting) the resources of a continent initially occupied by weaker societies, but also in the more fundamental sense of evading the demands of living closely and responsibly and creatively with other human beings. Nature offered, and Americans seized, a way of becoming a world unto themselves.

Perhaps any people so graced with such fortune would have responded similarly, but that truism (if it is a truism) does not mitigate the resulting and extreme elevation of the egoistic part of man over the social side of his nature. The result, as Turner realized, was that a "scorn of older society, impatience of its restraints and ideas, and indifference to its lessons, have accompanied the frontier." In this respect, of course, and it is a crucial one, the frontier is a cast of mind as well as a stretch of open territory. This attitude has been undeniably exhilarating in a psychological and philosophical sense, and has led to beneficial consequences in a materialistic calculus.

But the escape hatch of the frontier nevertheless directed Americans down a path that carried them ever further away from the great opportunity they enjoyed to create a truly human community. And, unless it is shortly modified and ultimately reversed, the subtle process which shifted the image of the frontier from the continent to an overseas economic empire will transfer it once again, this time to space itself, and the evasion will become literally projected to infinity.

For as Alfred North Whitehead has pointed out, the "bondage of the past" that Americans have been so desperate to escape is nothing more nor less than the challenge to transform human society "so as to make the original Christian ideas increasingly practicable for its individual members." Americans sought to evade this confrontation by using the frontier as a device whereby they could honor the injunction to "love thy neighbor as thyself" by merely executing their contractual, marketplace obligations to other individuals. Justice and equality, along with material well-being, were thereby defined as the result of successful business practices.

This essentially cramped and fundamentally negative and pessimistic conception of human life was of course a poor substitute for the ancient ideal of community. Thomas Hobbes undoubtedly understood that he would provoke great and outraged protest when he published his blunt handbook of the rules for constructing a society within those impoverished limits. But when modified by John Locke and Adam Smith so as to present a softer façade and a vague vision of Utopia, the essentials of Hobbes's system were accepted as the guidelines to enduring bliss.

For that matter, Hobbes himself pointed out the opening that Locke and Smith exploited in making his philosophy amenable to the general population. "Every man hath more or less liberty," Hobbes explained, "as he hath more or less space in which he employs himself." Locke and Smith rephrased the principle so that interminable expansion became the basis for eternal optimism and perpetual progress. "Liberty was lost," Smith warned, when expansion ceased. The classic American credo, "Bigger and Better," is little more than a banal formulation of that ancient rule. The arrogance of the Ego, that it could create a community through the unrestrained exercise of its liberty, was thus transformed into a pseudo-pious article of faith.

Whitehead was correct in characterizing this grandiose distortion of a profoundly pessimistic estimate of the nature of man into an apparently optimistic song of triumph as a "shallow philosophy," "a retrogression," and a "reactionary triumph of Periclean individualism." Even the extremely favorable circumstances enjoyed by Americans in the eighteenth and nineteenth centuries — a fantastically wealthy continent guarded by two ocean moats in an age of sailing ships — were insufficient to enable the system to generate any sustained success. But the belief itself was upheld as long as the frontier provided the chance to begin over again — and again and again. The commitment was so deep and intense, indeed, that the frontier was redefined as overseas expansion of the marketplace as the continent itself was occupied and that space exhausted. The world itself became the room required to swing the American Ego.

America did not become internationalist as it entered upon that particular new frontier at the turn of the twentieth century. It merely became super-nationalist. America built no communities. It simply projected itself into other areas. And today, as that expansion has been checked by the rise toward a parity of power by Russia and China, and as other areas increasingly reject the American intrusion (as for example, Cuba and Panama), it is apparent that the grand evasion has failed. It can be sustained, as with a leap into space, but it cannot produce the results it promises.

America has evaded nothing but the central issues. The short-run successes have served primarily to compound the fundamental difficulties. As revealed, for example, in the career of Henry L. Stimson, the duration of the triumphs has been shorter even than the lives of the men who initially engineered them. The exhilaration of the imperial victory in the Spanish-American War was transformed, within Stimson's own service as a policy-maker, into the fear and anxiety engendered by trying to sustain those earlier attitudes and policies—even with the power of a nuclear monoply—in the face of the opposition they had created. As Stimson so perceptively remarked, consciously or unconsciously using a classic idiom of the Frontier to make his point, the attempt to handle the Russians (and thereby the world) with *"this weapon rather ostentatiously on our hip"* would only increase the "suspicions" and "distrust" of the United States, and very probably lead to generally negative results.

Another illustration of how America has evaded nothing but the central issues is offered by President Lyndon Baines Johnson's State of the Union message of January 1964. Its form, style, and tone served primarily to document the continuing devolution of public prose toward the model evolved by the advertising industry as appropriate and effective for communicating with and controlling the captive audiences of the mass media. The short, flat, and monotonously simple and prosaic sentences approached a secular version of the catechism in which assertive, even aggressive, rhetorical pronouncements are presented as established truths and as reasoned, incontestable solutions to basic problems.

The substance of the speech was even more revealing of how the escape route of the frontier has turned out to be a circular path leading nowhere but back to the essential issues. The President defined four major problems facing the country. The search for peace was still unsuccessful, and had therefore to be continued with redoubled militance and increasingly deadly weapons. Unemployment not only existed, but threatened to continue its recent resurgence and become once again an overwhelming social problem. Despite imposing and ever increasing production totals, poverty remained so entrenched in America that it had become necessary to declare unconditional war on that blatant denial of the avowed effectiveness of the system. (The negative formulation of the recommended approach—"unconditional war"—is so revealing of a mental set as to be worth emphasizing. For it is at least conceivable that the issue of poverty could be dealt with through a call to honor the moral and social responsibilities of human relationships within a community.) And, finally, it was candidly admitted that the Negro still had not been granted elementary access to the ostensibly free marketplace more than a century after he had been formally and legally emancipated.

Noble though it was as a declaration of concern and as a manifesto of intent, the speech was even more significant as a catalogue of failures. This sobering thought is dramatized by even the most routine meditation on the reason that President Johnson was called upon to deliver that particular account of the society's unfulfilled promises. The reaction to the assassination of John Fitzgerald Kennedy offers a striking illustration of the extent to which Americans allow themselves to overlook the crucial difference between their beliefs about reality and reality itself. For the extent of the surprise, and the subsequent perplexity, about the assassination had no significant basis in the historical record. The act itself was not even remotely unique.

During the single generation between January 1933 and December 1963, assassins attempted to kill three of the four men who held the office of President of the United States. Such efforts were no novelty in American history prior to 1933, of course, but the markedly accelerated tempo of such acts indicated that the system was generating tensions faster than they were being resolved through the existing institutions and customs. While individuals who attempt the assassination of the highest leaders of the nation are, psychologically, severely disturbed men, each of these violent acts was clearly related to a structural crisis in the system itself.

President Franklin Delano Roosevelt, for example, was shot at during the height of the Great Depression by an unemployed man who avowed his deep anger over, and opposition to, the general inequities as well as to the specific breakdown of the system. The assassin's anarchism, far from representing or symbolizing some drastic and alien alternative, was merely a thoroughgoing projection of the existing order's central axioms concerning the primacy of the individual ego acting to preserve its sanctity and freedom of action.

The two subsequent attempts at assassination, those directed against Presidents Harry S. Truman and John Fitzgerald Kennedy, were intimately connected with the consequences of the imperial expansion initiated in the late 1880's and symbolized by the conquests of Puerto Rico and Cuba during the Spanish-American War. The men who assaulted Blair House in a frenzied effort to kill Truman consciously represented the final death agonies of Puerto Rican nationalism as the colony finally succumbed to the power of the United States and was transformed into a second-class state within the Metropolitan system.

Kennedy's death was even more indicative in that it symbolized the convergence of the domestic and the imperial failures. On the one hand, the act was a classic dramatization of the system's failure to extend its unbelievable largesse to all its citizens at home, and of its unwillingness to accept responsibility for the inability of the marketplace either to build a true community or to help the humans who are daily blighted and deformed by that failure. And, on the other hand, the act was intrinsically bound up with—and very probably triggered by—America's inability either to create a viable imperial relationship with Cuba or to grant the island the freedom to act within its own traditions and according to its own preferences.

Each of these episodes likewise reveals the frightening truth that the extreme achievements of and within American society are not only matched by extremes of failure, deprivation, and alienation within that society, but that there is no meaningful and consequential dialogue between the extremes. This breakdown of dialogue and reciprocal influence between the tiny community of power and the society-at-large indicates a withering away of representative government and its replacement by administered choices, paralleling the contraction of the free marketplace and its replacement by administered products and prices.

The alienation of the assassins and their lack of any significant participating share in the affairs of American society were extreme but they were not unique. The vast majority of Americans share varying degrees of such alienation and deprivation. "If one probes beneath the chrome-plated surface," Senator James William Fulbright recently acknowledged, "he comes inescapably to the conclusion that the American people by and large are not happy. . . .I believe. . .that America's trouble is basically one of aimlessness at home and frustration abroad."

This deepening crisis of increasing alienation, deprivation, and frustration was forecast over a century ago by Karl Marx. And of all the evasions in which Americans have indulged themselves, the most serious one is very probably their persistent flight from any intellectual and moral confrontation with Karl Marx. The tactics of escape employed in this headlong dash from reality would fill a manual of equivocation, a handbook of hairsplitting, and a guidebook to changing the subject. And if there is an American version of what has been called "the treason of the intellectuals," it lies not at all in their looking outside the United States to the Soviet Union as a beacon of hope for a better world, or as a model for emulation (for those acts were foursquare in the tradition of the frontier), but resides instead in their confusion of the reality of Marx with the reality of Russia.

For the most part, however, Americans have simply ignored Marx whenever it seemed possible to do so. At other times they have imprisoned socialists like Eugene Debs. And when those devices proved less than wholly successful, they declared Marx's ideas illegal so as to define a dialogue with him a crime under federal and state laws.

America's other principal technique of avoidance has been to re-define Marx as someone or something else that appeared easier to handle.

Thus Americans have made Marx into Lenin. And of course Lenin was wrong and also evil because he first weakened the position of the United States against Germany in World War I, and then challenged the United States to use its victory to translate its avowed ideals and promises into uncompromised actions and institutions.

Thus Americans have made Marx into Stalin. And of course Stalin was wrong and evil because he drove his country into the modern era, for which the United States had set the pattern, with a cruel and ruthless will that was particularly revolting to a people intensely concerned with forgetting the horror of the Civil War, the violence of the frontier, and the pain and suffering and death of their own industrial development.

And thus Americans have made Marx into the Soviet Union. And of course the Soviet Union is wrong and evil because it sustains the challenge first made by Marx (even if it does so in a gravely distorted form), because it challenges the viability and blocks the easy implementation of the American program for peace and prosperity, and perhaps most of all because it gives evidence of changing in ways that deny the American idea and image of it as a static and wholly evil society.

Americans have never confronted Karl Marx himself. We have never confronted his central theses about the assumptions, the costs, and the nature of capitalist society. We have never confronted his central insight that capitalism is predicated upon an overemphasis and exaltation of the individualistic, egoistic half of man functioning in a marketplace system that overrides and crushes the social, humanitarian half of man. We have never confronted his perception that capitalism is based upon a definition of man in the marketplace that defines the dialogue between men as a competitive struggle for riches and power. And we have never confronted his argument that capitalism cannot create a community in which how much men produce and own is less important than what they make, less important than their relationships as they produce and distribute those products, less important than what they are as men, and less important than how they treat each other.

Marx was a heretic. He was a citizen of Western civilization who challenged capitalism's ability to honor the West's historic and declared values and to achieve its avowed objectives. Far from denying those values, he militantly reasserted and defended them. To realize them, he called upon Western society to change its structure, its institutions, and its habits of thought and behavior and thereby create a true community. Marx was thus one of those most indispensable and annoying kind of men who function as critics and as consciences exhorting the rest of us to practice what we preach and to produce what we promise.

As is usually the case with heretics, Marx disturbed a great many people. In particular, he has persistently upset most Americans. Without any serious examination of the reality of Marx, they have concluded that he was entirely wrong. The American need to assert the vitality of the existing order has been father to the credo that the United States has proved that Marx was wrong, once and for all, in every essential respect.

This is a dangerously misleading evasion. It could conceivably be fatal. The reality of Marx offers insights and ideals that America desperately needs if it is to cope effectively with the reality of its present and projected problems, and if it is to realize its great potential. Hence this essay is an effort to initiate such a confrontation between the reality of Marx and the reality of America. In this way, it may be possible to bring the West's most challenging and creative heretic into the crucial dialogue about the future of the United States.

ONE

The Challenges Raised by Karl Marx

*W*e get no good
By being ungenerous, even to a book,
And calculating profits, — so much
    help
By so much reading. It is rather when
We gloriously forget ourselves and
    plunge
Soul-forward, headlong, into a book's
    profound,
Impassioned for its beauty and salt of
    truth —
'Tis then we get the right good from a
    book.

Elizabeth Barrett Browning,
Lady Geraldine's Courtship, Stanza 41

*O*NCE upon a time, even as recently as a century ago, Americans talked about America in positive terms. True enough, their conception of Utopia was cramped and confined within existing axioms and ideals, but their attitude was at least creative within those limits. Even in their negative moments, as when Thomas Jefferson could say no more for America than that it was the "last best hope" of the world, or when they admitted their shortcomings and criticized their mistakes, they were guided by a vision of a significantly better society.

In our time, by contrast, a debate on national purpose is a forced and labored exercise in journalistic commerce, political sophistry, and ideological casuistry. Even the participants acknowledge their boredom and embarrassment, and the enterprise slides unnoticed into bankruptcy. The supposedly great dialogue becomes just another statistic of business failure in a business society. The causes: insufficient capital and enterprise, and an unwillingness to innovate and take risks. Nobody involved has a concept of national purpose, let alone a program calculated to realize that vision, capable of exciting and engaging the population at large.

Consider another illustration. The era's most celebrated essay in political economy, John Kenneth Galbraith's imaginative report on his meanderings in a mythical land called *The Affluent Society,* is a complacent, inaccurate, misleading, and dangerously stultifying exercise in self-congratulation. The root meaning of *affluent* involves a free flow of plenty and abundance, and hence of wealth. Yet the sputtering, fluctuating performance of the American economy can hardly be characterized as an unfettered coursing, or as a free and easy operation—even during those periods when it has been assisted by the stimulus of war and cold war.

As for plenty and abundance, Galbraith simply discounts somewhere between 35 and 50 million human beings who exist under conditions of severe deprivation or outright poverty. These are people to whom the morning paper is "a luxury"; or who remember buying "my wife a pint of sherbet" as a rare and memorable event; or unemployed men aged thirty-seven who talk of themselves in stories like this: "I'll tell you something very funny. I hate wine. I almost puke every time I drink it. But if I didn't stay drunk, the chances are I'd kill myself." These people are not affluent. But Galbraith's term *society,* whatever its limitations as an ideal of human relationships, is an inclusive concept and does refer to everyone in the system.

As for wealth, Galbraith clearly and arbitrarily re-defines it to mean nothing more than the possession of a certain quantity of material goods and automatic or personal services. Yet the essential meaning of *wealth* has to do with an individual's effective, participating influence within his society. The great majority of Americans do not possess or exercise that kind of share or stake in contemporary society. From time to time, and in political as well as in economic affairs, a significant number of Americans register approval or disapproval of ideas or policies proposed — or already acted upon — by other people. But this does not constitute wealth in any meaningful sense.

Along with other examples of the same idiom (as, for example, Frederick Lewis Allen's *The Big Change* and Daniel Bell's *The End of Ideology*), Galbraith's rhetoric of triumphant achievement suggests — and sometimes indicates explicitly — that America has proved Karl Marx wrong in theory and in prophecy, and wrong everlastingly. In one form or another, this article of faith is accepted by men of all religions, races, creeds, functions, classes, incomes, statuses, I.Q.'s, and ideologies. For that matter, those who avow their radicalism seem at times to be shouting it a bit louder than anyone else.

This contemporary consensus on having proved Marx wrong does not involve any fundamentally new idea or attitude on the part of Americans. The formulation of the proposition in terms of Marx is clearly a product of the survival and progress of the Soviet Union, and of the appearance of other socialist and communist revolutions since the end of World War II. The central argument itself, however, is nothing more than a reassertion of the traditional doctrine of America's immaculate uniqueness. (It is worth noting that a people calling themselves unique thereby define themselves, perhaps only implicitly but nevertheless irrevocably, as either non-human, sub-human, or superhuman. Outsiders often perceive this corollary of the assertion of uniqueness, even if Americans overlook it, and it under-pins a good deal of their antagonism and resentment toward individual Americans and toward the United States.) In and of itself, the psy-chology of this almost obsessive assertion of uniqueness suggests that it may not be true. One has more than a hunch that we do insist too much.

For all these reasons, therefore, it seems the greater part of pru-dence to test the dogma by comparing the reality of Marx with the reality of America, instead of merely asserting that America has made Marx irrelevant. It is possible, for example, that Marx could be wrong and still offer insights relevant to contemporary problems. And it is conceivable that he was correct in defining the problems themselves, even though his prophecies may have been wrong.

Such an examination should direct itself to, and center itself upon, the broad nature and the principal themes of Marx's analysis of capitalism. *First,* the record of American diplomacy in the light of his analysis of the assumptions and dynamic nature of capitalist foreign relations. *Second,* the performance of the United States measured against his famous argument about the propensity of capitalism to produce increasing proletarianization and increasing misery. And *third,* the degree of American achievement in constructing society as an ethical and equitable and creative community. These issues lie at the heart of Marx's critique, and the claim to have proved him wrong can be sustained only if the facts reveal that the United States has transcended his description, analysis, and predictions.

Several general considerations should be kept in mind throughout such an evaluation, however, so as to counteract the habit of confusing the issues and faulting Marx on points not germane to the central line of his argument. Perhaps the most important of these involves his fidelity to the facts and his commitment to open-ended inquiry. Marx did discount, in his time, certain logical implications in his analysis of capitalism that later emerged as actual characteristics of the system. He also underestimated the impact or strength of some tendencies that were appearing at the end of his life. These are errors of judgment that can properly be criticized. But these mistakes do not necessarily destroy the broad lines of his argument.

Marx's work flowed from the methodological axiom that reality and change could be explained, and prognostications offered, by reference to the tension, conflict, and contradictions between the methods of production and the relations of production. By this he meant, fundamentally, the interaction between the way work could be done in any given circumstance and the way men organized themselves to do the work. Sticks and rocks demanded a certain kind of organization for cultivating fields, for example, and that organization begot new ideas about how men ought to be organized, as well as about how the ground might be tilled in different ways. Men acted on these ideas, either in favor of them or against them; that caused changes, and the new conditions generated more ideas.

Men therefore made their own history, but they did so within the limits of existing reality (which of course included old as well as new ideas). It should be clear, though it is often overlooked, that Marx understood and acknowledged the influence of ideas. He did argue, however, that basic ideas changed only very slowly. Hence he insisted that the economic rules, practices, habits, and relationships created by one such set of ideas became and remained the predominant — and even an almost independent — factor in a given situation until new ideas changed the system.

This is often misunderstood as saying that all human action can be, or even must be, explained as flowing from individual, personal economic motives. Marx was no such fool as that. He was quite aware that men could and did act from economic motives, but he also realized that they could and did act on the much broader basis of thinking that the whole network of political and social relationships depended upon maintaining certain economic patterns. They could act, that is, to sustain the marketplace per se as well as an entrepreneur within the marketplace. And Marx explicitly acknowledged the role of passion and chance in affecting the *short-run* development of the system.

Given this basic approach, Marx was intellectually incorruptible. As he put it time and time again, it was the facts — not the conclusions already demonstrated or the wishes of the student — that determined the analysis in each specific case. "I am not a Marxist!" he once cried in disgust and anguish over self-appointed followers who applied a schematic version of his complex analytic approach to the facts and produced brittle explanations and stereotyped predictions. "One will never succeed," Marx flatly asserted, "with the open sesame of an historico-philosophical theory, of which the supreme virtue consists in its being *supra-historical*." Marx's assumptions, axioms, and methods, and his broad analysis, rather than any particular or detailed prognostication he offered, are the crucial elements of his contribution.

It is worth re-emphasizing that Marx did not neglect or discount ideas. This is one of the most common criticisms of him. Its proponents claim he made man into a machine guided by a kind of economic radar. This is simply wrong. He was unequivocal on the point that men could entertain ideas that were broader than those derived from their specific economic role or position. A radical, revolutionary "class consciousness," he pointed out, "can of course also rise in other classes from the observation of the situation of [the proletarian] class."

Marx could not discount ideas for the simple reason that he was principally concerned with the central axioms and dynamic propensities of capitalist development. Indeed, one might argue with considerable effect that it was his very overemphasis on the power of ideas that led him repeatedly, and in a way that contradicted another part of his analysis of ideas, to underestimate the time required for the full evolution of the dynamic features he defined as being the causal engines of the capitalist process. He was very prone to assume that men would perceive the true nature of their condition, and proceed to improve it, much more quickly than they actually did — or have.

Marx's foreshortened sense of time did have the effect of distorting some of his specific projections and predictions. But it seems fair to point out that the problem of understanding and being right about time is a difficulty that plagues all historians and social scientists. Even economists have trouble with time. Those who dismiss Marx have not met this challenge any more effectively than he did. If anything, they have foreshortened time even more drastically. Marx talked about capitalism over a period of at least five centuries, whereas his critics dismiss him as hopelessly wrong on the evidence of less than one. For that matter, most Americans who dispense with him as being irrelevant base their argument on the events of an infinitesimal period between 1941 and 1955.

Finally, it is pertinent to recall Marx's uninhibited praise of capitalist performance. He never intimated, let alone asserted, that capitalism was an unmitigated failure or an unrelieved agony. This seems particularly relevant in connection with America, where the achievement has been great — even if the resources and the favorable circumstances have been grandiose.

The bourgeoisie, Marx commented quite without niggardliness, "has played a most revolutionary part. . . .It has been the first to show what man's activity can bring about. It has accomplished wonders far surpassing Egyptian pyramids, Roman aqueducts, and Gothic cathedrals; it has conducted expeditions that put in the shade all former Exoduses of nations and crusades. . . .[It] has created more massive and more colossal productive forces than have all preceding generations together. . . .What earlier century had even a presentiment that such productive forces slumbered in the lap of social labor?" And, furthermore, the bourgeoisie "has given a cosmopolitian character to production and consumption in every country. . . .National one-sidedness and narrow-mindedness become more and more impossible, and from the numerous national and local literatures, there arises a world literature."

With these often neglected aspects of Marx clearly in mind, and hopefully fixed therein for the duration of this discussion, it is appropriate to begin an evaluation of his critique of capitalism by comparing his general argument about foreign relations with the record of American foreign policy.

TWO

*T*he Expansion of the Marketplace and Capitalist Foreign Relations

*W*hen the produce of any particular branch of industry exceeds what the demand of the country requires, the surplus must be sent abroad. . . .It is only by means of such exportation that this surplus can acquire a value sufficient to compensate the labour and expense of producing it.

The revenue of a trading and manufacturing country must, other things being equal, always be much greater than that of one without trade or manufactures. . . .A trading and manufacturing country, therefore, naturally purchases with a small part of its manufactured produce a great part of the rude produce of other countries; while, on the contrary, a country without trade and manufactures is generally obliged to purchase, at the expense of a great part of its rude produce, a very small part of the manufactured produce of other countries. . . .The inhabitants of the one must always enjoy a much greater quantity of subsistence than what their own lands, in the actual state of their cultivation, could afford. The inhabitants of the other must always enjoy a much smaller quantity.

Adam Smith,
The Wealth of Nations

*M*ARX never prepared a separate, formal study of capitalist foreign relations, and no one has ever collected his scattered discussions of the subject into one co-ordinated volume. V. I. Lenin's famous essay on *Imperialism* is a significant document in its own idiom, but it has little value as a basis for evaluating Marx. The same is true of the neglected study by Nikolai Bukharin, *Imperialism and World Economy,* although it provides a somewhat better outline of Marx's own ideas. It seems wise, therefore, to review the main elements of Marx's analysis as he offered it in his own studies of capitalism.

One of the central features of capitalism, Marx argued, was its splitting of the economy into two principal parts. This "cleavage between town and country" was not complete, of course, but the reciprocal relationship between them was heavily imbalanced in favor of the town, or Metropolitan, sector. Marx was here following Adam Smith, the master theorist of capitalism, as well as the facts he gathered in his own study of the system. This was one of the most important instances in which the theory and the practice of capitalism coincided.

Another such example involved the continued expansion of the marketplace, first within a country and then beyond its boundaries. The never-ending necessity to accumulate additional surplus value, or capital, a process which was essential for the system as well as to the individual businessman, meant that this market "must, therefore, be continually extended." Without such expansion the economic system would stagnate at a certain level of activity, and the political and social system based upon it would suffer severe strains leading either to a caste society upheld by force or to revolution. Hence "the real task of bourgeois society," Marx explained, "is the establishment of the world market. . .and a productive system based on this foundation."

As it crossed the national boundary, this process transformed "the cleavage between town and country" into "the colonial system." The town became the developed, industrial Metropolis, while the country became the backward, underdeveloped society. It follows both logically and from the evidence that the periodic crises created and suffered by capitalism intensified the drive to expand the market. "The conquest of new markets and the more thorough exploitation of the old ones," Marx pointed out, served as the principal means whereby the internal crisis in the Metropolis "seeks to balance itself."

Concerning both the normal and the crisis situations, Marx was typically succinct and non-euphemistic in describing the central feature of this expansion of the marketplace. "The favored country recovers more labor in exchange for less labor." It is worth re-emphasizing, moreover, that Adam Smith reached the identical conclusion, and based his entire theory and strategy of capitalist success on this essentially imbalanced relationship between the Metropolis and the country society.

Such expansion of the marketplace is directly and explicitly relevant to an understanding of American foreign relations. It offers, to begin with, a good many insights into the major periods of American diplomacy. The first of these eras began in the middle of the eighteenth century and culminated in the 1820's. The increasing British efforts after 1750 to control and limit the existing American marketplace, its further agrarian expansion westward, and its increasing share in international trade, led to a confrontation with the colonists that lies at the heart of the American Revolution.

Similar British attempts to restrict American territorial expansion after independence had been won, and to set limits upon America's international trade (which antagonized the surplus-producing farmers as well as other groups), promoted and accelerated and intensified the nationalism which led to the War of 1812. And the American push into the Floridas, and into the trans-Mississippi region, was obviously expansionist in origin and purpose. The vision of a great trade with South America and Asia, while not as central to these movements as the concern for land, was nevertheless a significant part of the continuing pressure to expand the marketplace that culminated in the Trans-Continental Treaty of 1819 with Spain.

Throughout this period, moreover, the same underlying thrust to expand the marketplace defined the basic character of American policy toward the Indians. The drive to dispossess the natives of their land, and the campaign to remove all restrictions on trade with the various tribes, combined to drive the Indians further westward while at the same time subverting any efforts to integrate them as full citizens into the white man's society and weakening their ability to resist further encroachments.

In a similar way, Marx's emphasis on the expansion of the marketplace offers major—and in many respects still unexploited—perceptions concerning the struggle between various elements of the country during the 1840's and 1850's to organize the marketplace along one of three alternate axes: a North-South, a South-West, or a North-West alliance. The psychology of fear that became so apparent in all sections of the nation on the eve of the Civil War, for example, is directly related to this increasingly intense conflict.

Farmers in the region north of the Ohio River not only manifested an active desire to control the national government and the Western territories for their own benefit, but developed a corresponding antagonism toward other groups and regions which appeared to be blocking their attempts to win that predominance. Southerners expressed similar hopes and fears, as did still other groups in the

Northeastern part of the country. As the economic integration between the Northeastern "town" and the food-producing Northwestern "country" became stronger than an earlier relationship between the Eastern Metropolis and the Southern raw material producing "country," Southerners increasingly defined themselves as members of a potentially independent system sustained and strengthened through connections with non-American Metropolitan areas.

The formerly regional conflicts thus gradually changed into a struggle between two giant sections over the issue of which was to control the trans-Mississippi West. Both blocs viewed that area as what today would be called an underdeveloped, potentially neocolonial resource that would guarantee their respective prosperity and security. At bottom, both sections viewed slavery as an economic phenomenon that would determine the outcome of the marketplace struggle for final victory. Ultimately, of course, slavery became both a symbol of that conflict and a moral and ideological banner for both sides. If slavery be said to have caused the Civil War, however, it must also be said that it did so more in its economic sense than in its moral respect. For the general response to the abolitionist minority (both positive and negative) was grounded in the economic fears of Northerners and Southerners who saw themselves first of all as combatants in a desperate struggle to control the continental marketplace.

The postwar conflicts between the Eastern Metropolis and the Southern and Western agrarian sectors of the economy can most fruitfully be approached as a clear illustration of the validity of the emphasis placed on "the cleavage between town and country" by Smith and Marx. This provides by far the most accurate guideline to any understanding and interpretation of the Granger, Alliance, and Populist movements. Even a viable psychological interpretation of these protest movements must be grounded upon such a structural analysis.

The general drive to expand the marketplace during these same years of the late nineteenth century provided the primary energy for the American economic move outward into Europe, Africa, Latin America, and Asia. That expansion has been sustained and intensified in the twentieth century. Nobody but Americans thrust world power upon the United States. It came as a direct result of this determined push into the world marketplace. John D. Rockefeller's comment on the policy of Standard Oil typifies the attitude of both centuries. "Dependent solely upon local business," he explained in 1899, "we should have failed years ago. We were forced to extend our markets and to seek for export trade."

Since the farmer was a capitalist entrepreneur (a vital consideration often neglected or discounted in narrowly psychological interpretations of his behavior), Marx's analysis provides an insight into the policies and actions of the agrarians that most commentators have overlooked. If Marx is correct, that is, then the evidence ought to reveal the farmers participating in the expansionist movement as their production outran domestic consumption. The documents show precisely that: the American farmer's concern with overseas markets played a significant part in initiating and sustaining the momentum of the idea and the practice of such expansion.

Beginning in the early 1880's, the farmers' turn to export markets led directly to diplomatic encounters with England, France, Austria-Hungary, and Germany. It also prompted specific urban business interests, such as the railroads, the flour millers, the meat packers, and the implement manufacturers, to follow the lead of the farmers and undertake their own expansionist efforts. And, more generally, urban business leaders increasingly looked to agricultural export figures as a reliable index of general economic activity.

Politicians likewise responded, and the campaign for reciprocity treaties drew almost as much support from certain agrarian groups (as with Secretary of State James G. Blaine's efforts in 1890 to win reciprocity agreements with Cuba and other food-importing nations) as from the manufacturers. This involvement in the world marketplace also played a central role in the agrarian campaign for unlimited coinage of silver at a ratio of 16 to 1. The farmers, and their leaders like William Jennings Bryan, argued that free coinage would free America from economic control by Great Britain and other European powers and give the United States economic supremacy in the world marketplace. This militant and expansive economic nationalism, which stemmed directly from the experience of the farmers in having to deal through Liverpool and London, not only provided a surprising amount of support for building a new and big navy and taking Hawaii, but was a very significant factor in the coming of the Spanish-American War.

Marx's particular emphasis on foreign policy as a way to generate recovery in the context of economic crisis is also verified by American behavior. The trans-Appalachian depression that developed between 1808 and 1811, and which hit the farmers hard, had a direct causative connection with the agitation that elected the War Hawks and led to the War of 1812. Expansion into Mexico began in the downturn after the War of 1812, and matured into an imperial clash ultimately involving war during the panics and the depression of the late 1830's. The same pattern appears in the late 1860's and the 1870's, though it is somewhat camouflaged by taking the form, at least primarily, of the North's extension of its economic control over the South and the West.

Americans again began to react more explicitly and generally to depressions by turning to economic expansion during the business troubles of the 1880's, a decade when surplus production began to pose a problem in some industries as well as in agriculture. This response crystallized during the panic and depression of the 1890's and prompted the appearance of a good many general theories about the necessity of such expansion. Such ideas played a double role: they served as an explanation of what was happening, and they offered a solution for the difficulties of the system. As a result, they were a primary causative force in the imperial expansion of the period.

This emphasis on overseas economic expansion, through both exports and investments, was an integral part of the New Deal program for recovery from the Great Depression. And it was the central theme of the discussions during 1943 – 1945 concerning the best way to handle the depression that was expected to develop at the end of World War II. The same approach has been increasingly emphasized during the series of postwar recessions. The New Frontier's stress on the expansion of exports and the creation of regional markets tied to the American system is candidly explained and defended as a solution for the specific difficulties of the domestic economy and the more general problems incident to the breakdown of the nineteenth-century imperial system.

Marx recognized and understood that the imperial relationship that evolved out of such economic expansion could take several forms. One of these is colonialism, which involves the seizure or conquest of empty, or lightly populated, real estate and the subsequent transfer of other people into the new area. It is accompanied by direct and extensive controls over the new society, as well as over the displaced or conquered population. Americans take great pride, of course, in denying any colonial blemish upon their historical record. This case is debatable even if colonialism is defined or thought of, as it usually is by Americans, as involving action across the open sea.

But there is no serious justification for making the crossing of water a necessary condition of colonialism. The essential definition is the control of territory and resources, and the displacement, re-establishment, and control of human beings. American policy toward the Indian, and toward the Negro from 1650 to 1863, certainly satisfies those criteria and therefore belies the assertion that the United States has never been a colonial power. It is customary and accurate to talk about the Negro during those years as a slave, but slavery is only the most extreme form of colonial exploitation. In any event, the Negro was transported across the sea in the course of being colonized.

There was also a significant degree of colonialism involved in the economic and political controls exercised by the American Metropolis over the Western territories. Jefferson's attitude toward the non-English settlers in the region acquired through the Louisiana Purchase is symbolic, not only of the discrepancy between his rhetoric and his policy, but also of the general attitude of the East toward the new settlements across the mountains. The foreigners could acquiesce or leave, Jefferson announced; otherwise force would be used against them.

The process by which the settlements beyond the Appalachians were ultimately accepted as full members of the federal commonwealth does not offer as great an exception to the usual colonial pattern as latter-day Americans are inclined to assume. For one thing, the final agreement to admit such areas as states was not achieved without overt resistance by the territories against being treated as colonies. The agitation of the 1780's, for example, had a great deal to do with overcoming Easterners who wanted to handle the trans-Appalachian region as a colony in the traditional British manner.

In the final plan, moreover, the Metropolis was given many

explicit controls over a territory until it was admitted as a state, and these opened the way for outsiders to establish their power and authority in less formal ways. It often took a generation (if not longer) for the new state to break free of the resulting institutionalized influence. Nor was statehood granted by the Metropolis with any noticeable dispatch. After the Civil War, for example, only two territories (Nebraska and Colorado) gained legal equality during a period of twenty-four years. As might be imagined, this artificial and protracted delay reinforced and intensified other causes involved in the West's antagonism and resistance toward outsiders.

A second kind of imperial relationship that Marx recognized and discussed is the form of administrative colonialism evolved by the British in India during and after the 1850's. This pattern is characterized by the effective control by an outside minority, through force and the threat of force, of alien territory and population, and by its concurrent establishment of economic predominance. It does not involve, as with colonialism per se, the large-scale transfer of population under the direction and control of the Metropolis. There is emigration from the Metropolis, but it is strictly limited both in numbers and direct function. Its object is to provide a military force in being in support of the leadership necessary for the effective control and management of the political economy of the subject society. The emigrants thus comprise an absolute and a relatively small group of army and naval personnel, political administrators, and economic directors. The success of the system, and of the agents of the Metropolis, is measured by the degree to which absentee control of crucial decisions is institutionalized within a framework of native self-government in local affairs, and routinely maintained domestic political and social peace.

American administrative colonialism appears most classically in the cases of Cuba and the Philippines. All the features of the system were apparent: the colony's own internal cleavage between town and country, its imbalanced, limited, and skewed development, and the improvement purchased at the price of drastic costs in human and material resources, and in harmful consequences to the social fabric itself. The same pattern, with variations appropriate to the circumstances, has emerged in American relations with Liberia and many Latin-American countries, such as Nicaragua and Guatemala. And the current American relationships with Okinawa, South Korea, and Vietnam follow the main outlines of such administrative colonial empire.

The third principal form of the imperial relationship emerges in the evolution of the inherent nature of the marketplace connection between a Metropolis and a backward, underdeveloped region or society. It arises out of the imbalance between the two societies which produces the situation so aptly described by Adam Smith: "The revenue of a trading and manufacturing country must, other things being equal, always be much greater than that of one without trade or manufactures. . . .A country without trade and manufactures is generally obliged to purchase, at the expense of a great part of its rude produce, a very small part of the manufactured produce of other countries." Or as described by Karl Marx: "The favored country recovers more labor in exchange for less labor." Or, to phrase it in the language of our own time, the price received by the underdeveloped country for its goods and services does not suffice to pay for the goods and services it requires to initiate and sustain its own development. For that matter, in many cases the prices set by the Metropolis for such goods decline so much that the loss to the underdeveloped country is not even made up by grants or loans provided by the Metropolis.

Even under the most favorable circumstances, therefore, the gap between the rich and the poor remains constant or decreases only in tiny and sporadic increments. At worst (and more usually), the increases take the form of creeping impoverishment in the poorer nation. Or, as Marx put it, in a kind of increasing misery and increasing proletarianization. It is essential to realize that, whatever the evidence indicates as to increasing misery within the Metropolis, the facts of the world capitalist marketplace support Marx's analysis. He was correct. The poor are poorer and more miserable.

While force is periodically employed, and formal agents from the Metropolis occasionally take a direct hand in managing the affairs of the weaker society, neither action is a routine, institutionalized part of this variant of the imperial relationship. British historians have recently used the phrases, "the imperialism of free trade" and "informal empire," to describe this pattern, and their suggestions seem astute, accurate, and convenient. As Marx clearly understood, the system evolves from the basic capitalist conception of the market and the marketplace as the Metropolis expands into the backward area.

The marketplace is an integrated, two-way relationship involving access to raw materials as well as export markets for goods, services, and investment capital. Marx understood these reasons that lay behind the expansionist arguments developed by American farmers and industrial leaders. They pointed out the marginal utility of foreign operations and explained why it was rational to sell at a loss overseas in order to avoid the economic and social costs of shutting down when the domestic demand was satisfied. In addition to saving capital and avoiding labor unrest, such practices offered an effective strategy for entering and winning control of foreign markets.

American foreign relations since 1895 provide the central historical illustration of this kind of imperial expansion. The informal empire of the United States in the twentieth century offers an example of the character, dynamism, and consequences of the capitalist marketplace that is even purer in form and substance than the one provided by British expansion after the middle of the nineteenth century. The famous Open Door Notes of 1899 and 1900 were consciously and brilliantly formulated on the assumption that America possessed the necessary and overwhelming economic power vis-à-vis other advanced industrial powers, as well as the weaker, poorer countries, and on the conviction that Adam Smith was correct in holding that such strength would enable the United States to control the world marketplace if it was defined as a fair field with favor to none.

Given this belief in the fundamental economic preponderance of their system, American policy-makers designed their imperial strategy with a view to creating and maintaining the conditions which would enable their nation's power to produce the desired economic and political victories. Since they viewed war as the great disrupter of economic progress, and as the nightrider of political and social regression, their broad objective was to establish rules of the game which would prevent the struggle in the marketplace from becoming a trial by arms.

The Open Door Notes sought to do this in Asia (and, later, in other regions, such as Africa) by committing America's industrial rivals to the following principles of policy and action: (1) a prohibition on further division and colonization of such areas as China; (2) existing and subsequent regulations within established spheres of interest to apply equally to all competitors; and (3) equal opportunity to be afforded to all rivals in all future economic activity.

While the strategy did not succeed in preventing subsequent wars, it is crucial to realize that the United States entered such conflicts to defend and to re-establish the Open Door Policy. In an important degree, moreover, America was drawn into those wars because of antagonisms arising out of the effectiveness of its performance within the limits set by the principles of the Open Door Policy. This was true in the positive sense of American economic penetration and influence in the world marketplace after 1900, as well as in the negative sense that the Open Door Policy appeared to competitors as an obstacle to their own progress. In this respect, at any rate, the policy was effective enough in its actual or potential economic operation to subvert its political and military objectives.

The evolution and adoption of the Open Door Policy involved one of the truly majestic ironies of American—and perhaps even Western—history. Men like Theodore Roosevelt and Henry Cabot Lodge initially favored a vigorous kind of administrative colonialism as the proper strategy of American expansion. Not unjustly, therefore, they came to be known as Imperialists. Their critics and opponents, men like Andrew Carnegie, William Jennings Bryan, and Edward Atkinson, claimed and were known by the label of Anti-Imperialists. This likewise was true and fair enough as a description of their position on traditional colonialism, or even formal and extensive administrative colonialism.

But the Anti-Imperialists were actually men who understood and advocated the very kind of informal empire that Adam Smith and Karl Marx maintained was created by the inherent imbalance of the marketplace relationship between the advanced industrial Metropolis and the poor, backward, agrarian societies. To begin with, the Anti-Imperialists argued that the economic and other institutional requirements of colonialism or widespread administrative colonialism would slow down and limit the accumulation of capital at home, would progressively limit essential bourgeois freedoms, and would breed social unrest. They added that such a strategy of expansion would also encourage and sustain resistance movements in the dependencies and lead to wars with other advanced nations. Taken together, such consequences would be very apt to subvert economic and political liberty at home, and might even bring about the destruction of the empire itself. To avoid such dangers, yet enjoy the necessary expansion of the marketplace, the Anti-Imperialists rested their strategy of empire on the very principle that Adam Smith advanced.

The Anti-Imperialists and Smith were correct. The Open Door Policy worked magnificently for half a century — surely as effectively as the European forms of colonialism and administrative colonialism. American economic power expanded throughout the world, into the other advanced countries as well as into the underdeveloped regions (including European colonies and spheres of interest), and came ultimately and literally to dominate the world capitalist marketplace. And, measured either in absolute terms or relatively against the performance of the older patterns of empire, the United States was required to employ but small amounts of force between 1900 and 1950 in order to maintain its imperial relationship with the weaker countries. Within the assumptions of the system, American economic power was deployed with considerably more astuteness, and managed with more finesse and sophistication, than either its advocates or its critics are often prone to admit. In addition to the huge profits returned to the United States, the result was the creation of a pattern of domestic politics within the "country" side of the empire that sustained pro-American rulers in power for the great majority of the years since 1900.

But Karl Marx was also correct. The inherent drive within the advanced countries to accumulate capital and to expand and control the marketplace, and the resulting increasing proletarianization and misery in the subject half of the empire, has led to more and increasingly violent conflict. American entry into World War I was at bottom predicated upon the conclusion, reached by both top economic and high political leaders, that the United States could not risk being excluded from what appeared to be the probable reorganization of the world marketplace on terms that would seriously restrict, if not actually subvert, the operation of the Open Door Policy.

Both the Allies and the Central Powers had made it clear by 1916 that they would transform a military and political victory into an economic system strongly favorable to themselves. Wilson's emphasis on his famous Fourteen Points, and his insistence on the Covenant of the League of Nations, involved far more than transcendental idealism. Those programs were designed to apply the axioms of the Open Door Policy to the world and, through the crucial Article X of the Covenant, to guarantee their observance for an indefinite future. The same considerations, even more explicitly avowed, lie at the heart of American involvement in World War II and the Cold War.

America's increasing opposition to Germany and Italy began not with the attacks on Czechoslovakia or Poland, but in connection with basic Axis economic policy (such as barter agreements in place of open marketplace transactions) as early as 1933, and in response to German penetration of Latin-American economic affairs during that decade. Germany's increasing resort to force to extend the sway of such ideas and policies, and others including racial persecution, carried the economic and ideological conflict into the military arena before Japan's attack on Pearl Harbor. From the very beginning, moreover, American leaders openly acknowledged that the tension with Japan was created by the decision to uphold and enforce the principles of the Open Door Policy in China and southeastern Asia in the face of Japanese expansion.

Antagonism toward the Soviet Union involved the same issues in an even more central and unqualified manner. This struggle, which had begun in 1917 and 1918, involved an outright rejection by the Soviets of the cardinal principles of the capitalist marketplace. The United States never fully reconciled itself to this withdrawal by Russia from the capitalist world. In the more narrow and explicit sense, this opposition manifested itself at the end of World War II in an openly proclaimed American determination to preserve and institutionalize the principles of the Open Door Policy in northeastern Asia and in eastern Europe. The Soviet Union's avowed willingness to negotiate particular and more limited rights for the capitalist world in those regions was never explored in any serious, sustained manner. The United States defined the choice as lying between an acceptance of the principles of the Open Door Policy or a condition of opposition and antagonism.

None of this means (in any of the three instances) that the United States entered upon war simply to make money. Certain freedoms and liberties are essential to capitalists and capitalism, even though capitalists and capitalism are not essential to freedom and liberty. There is no discrepancy, therefore, in going to war for a free marketplace and going to war to defend, secure, and even extend the particular freedoms and liberties associated with such a marketplace political economy. But if either war had been fought solely for those freedoms and liberties, then the condition of the underdeveloped part of the world would have been quite different as early as 1920. And its circumstances would have changed much more rapidly, and with considerably less violence against the advanced Metropolitan countries, after the victory in 1945.

Hence none of these actions involved either a series of terrible conspiracies or a kind of narrow, crude economic motivation or determinism on the part of American leaders or their constituency. All parties had a sincere and practical commitment to the kind of freedom inherent in the Open Door Policy per se, and in the informal empire constructed by the United States between 1898 and 1950. The issue is not how bad or evil Americans were, but rather the far more profound and human theme of their tragic inability to realize their desire for peace and freedom so long as they declined to modify seriously the principles of possessive individualism that lie at the heart of capitalism.

As far as America's informal empire itself is concerned, the case of Cuba serves perfectly — if horribly — to illustrate the validity of Marx's analysis. Or, for that matter, the accuracy of Adam Smith's argument. To Marx's axiom about who takes more labor from whom, add his principle that "violent eruptions are naturally more likely to occur in the extremities of the bourgeois organism than in its heart," and top it off with his conclusion that the ideals of the capitalist fight a generally losing battle with the economic axioms of the system. The result is a definition of, and a set of major insights into, the principal features of Cuban-American relations from 1895 to the present. Marx was not primarily concerned to predict when the convulsion would occur, or who would ride its first wave. He was engaged in explaining what would happen, and why it would occur, if the Metropolis continued to act on the principles of the marketplace in its relationships with a colonial or otherwise dependent society. The origins and evolution of the Cuban Revolution, and the nature and course of its confrontation with the United States, verify the central themes of his analysis.

The Cuban missile crisis of 1962 offers an international example of Marx's fundamental argument that a change in the forces of production ultimately causes a change in the relations of production. In the confrontations of war and cold war, of course, the means of production are ultimately defined in military terms. During the years that the United States enjoyed a monopoly or a significant advantage in nuclear weapons, from 1945 to 1955, it unilaterally established and in large measure maintained the ground rules for international relations in the atomic age.

There were exceptions, particularly in China, that provided clear warnings that this vast preponderance of productive power did not provide the United States with an ability to control every situation. The policy was based on a far too narrow, and even typically market-place, definition of power. It provided an excellent illustration of the way in which the mind concerned with commodities discounts the significance of people. The instruments of power were confused with the sources of power.

The signs indicating the dangers in this outlook were largely ignored until the Russians developed the same productive forces and the same instruments of power. Even then, however, the evidence continued to be generally discounted for a considerable period. Americans continued to make a fetish of producing the commodity of the atom and hydrogen bombs, arguing quite irrationally that the power to kill everybody twice or thrice gave them more security than only being able to do so once. The situation took on the characteristics of a macabre extension of the national attitude toward buying multiple automobiles. Thorstein Veblen might have discussed the phenomenon under the heading of the urge to conspicuous annihilation.

Then came the Cuban Revolution. It was an example of the impotence of nuclear supremacy that could not be evaded or rationalized away. American control of the island had been too obvious for too long a time, and the absurdity of vaporizing the revolution in order to save trade and investments was so evident as to be humorous despite the frustration. Americans sensed, when they did not realize it more explicitly, that the revolution was the product of their own administrative colonialism and informal empire. Even the Pavlovian exercises in explaining it as the work of a communist conspiracy were feeble and generally unimpressive examples of casuistry.

The first direct attempt to destroy the revolution employed the strategy of using conventional weapons inside what was thought to be the womb of safety provided by nuclear predominance. But the strength of the revolution foiled that American effort to combine superficial morality and rhetorical righteousness with secret malice. The subsequent nuclear showdown with the Russians was a direct consequence of that unsuccessful effort to square the circle. Cuban leaders became convinced that the United States would try again with vastly greater forces. This may not have been true, but they declined to risk their revolution on the word of an American administration that had already acted differently than it had talked.

On the surface, it is true, the productive forces of the United States emerged triumphant in the resulting confrontation with the Soviet Union. "The other fellow blinked," as the story goes. But as Secretary of State Dean Rusk later acknowledged, the United States for the first time caught a glimpse of the true nature of nuclear reality. The Soviets withdrew their missiles, but the United States gradually realized that it, the world's greatest Metropolis, had become a colony. A colony, that is to say, of the vast forces of production that it had created and put on the marketplace.

For in a profound sense, the increasing recognition of the necessity of co-existence that dates from the Cuban missile crisis stands as proof of Marx's central thesis that the productive forces will ultimately determine the relations of production. No single entrepreneur can impose his will on the economic marketplace if he is blocked by an element of comparable strength, save at a price so dear as to be self-destructive. Neither can one superpower impose its will upon the international nuclear marketplace if it is matched by another superpower, save at the cost of the very influence it is seeking to enlarge. There is considerable evidence, moreover, that one of the main reasons Soviet leaders placed their weapons in Cuba was to dramatize this truth to the United States.

It is conceivable that, despite that encounter, the United States will continue trying to prove Marx wrong by sustaining the essential structure and attitudes of the Cold War. That approach reveals a powerful inherent propensity to devolve into nuclear war. It is a dynamism that is not effectively checked, let alone redirected, by mere changes in the rhetoric or the means employed in connection with the existing policy. Even if the policy somehow avoided nuclear war, America would not really have proved that Marx was wrong. Another decade of cold war, even more sophisticated and more gentlemanly cold war, would destroy capitalism in any meaningful — let alone American — sense. The result would be a form of non-violent, totalitarian state managerialism that would make C. Wright Mills's power elite look like the founding fathers of Jacksonian Democracy.

These considerations may serve to clarify a generally misunderstood aspect of Marx's theory and analysis. To accept the proposition that changes in the forces of production lead inexorably to changes in the relations of production is not to accept as a corollary that those changes will inevitably take one course or pattern. Marx held that men make their own history within the limits they create for themselves, but he never abstracted intellect or volition from man himself.

He acknowledged, for example, that it was possible for an advanced capitalist country to make the transition to socialism without a violent social upheaval. "We do not deny that there are countries, like England and America, . . . where the worker may attain his object by peaceful means." Even if co-existence is thought of wholly within a Marxian framework, which is most certainly not necessary, it is false to assume or fear that the result is pre-ordained by some inexorable superhuman law. To accept the necessity of co-existence is not to bow fatalistically to the idea that everyone has to embrace communism as defined and practiced by Lenin, Stalin, Mao, or Khrushchev. Those models comprise but a tiny percentage of the alternatives. The acceptance of co-existence actually opens up a wide range of possibilities, whereas the insistence on trying to preserve the conventional wisdom of the Cold War drives America deeper into a cul-de-sac.

Within a year after the Cuban missile crisis created some recognition of these considerations and possibilities, the perceptive and courageous Senator George McGovern boldly challenged American leaders to adapt their ideas and their policies to the new reality. "We need," he said, "a thoroughly honest discussion and debate, not so much about competing weapons systems, but rather about the basic postulates of our defense strategy. . . .What is the mounting arms race doing to our freedom and the quality of our lives?. . .Are we following a blueprint for peace or racing toward annihilation?" He then bluntly asserted that "the United States now has a stockpile of nuclear weapons in excess of any conceivable need." Nor did he shrink from pointing out that the national fetish concerning nuclear commodities had failed to prevent the rise of structural unemployment, and that it had left America with a shopping list of urgent social and humanitarian needs that would take years—if not decades—to fill.

In the realm of foreign affairs, at least, the United States has not proved that Karl Marx was wrong. America has been a colonial power. America has practiced administrative colonialism on a significant scale. America has built an informal empire of massive proportions. And America is now face to face with the proof of Marx's thesis that such empires create their own increasingly effective opposition both from within and from without.

It would appear to be the greater part of wisdom, to say nothing of safety, to admit that Marx was right. That would enable us to invest our intellectual and psychological and moral capital in an imaginative effort to adjust our foreign policy to the very reality we have done so much to create. We could begin, for example, by getting straight on the actual and limited power of money. True, money can buy some governments some of the time. But money cannot even buy some governments all of the time, let alone all of the governments all of the time.

This limitation arises from the nature of governments. Governments are made of and by people. This is the case whether or not other people make their governments in the same way we Americans make ours. And money does not buy people. It only buys their labor or the product of their labor. Hence when they produce a new government, all we have to show for our money is the old-model government which has been dropped from the assembly line.

Having come to terms with the limited power of money to buy success in foreign affairs, we might then confront the problem of how best to transcend the inequities of the international capitalist marketplace. Here the first problem is to relax enough to stop reading the headlines as though they were bulletins on the state of our manhood. This is a magnificent epoch. Billions of people are beginning to control their own societies for the first time in centuries. We should relax enough to be exhilarated when they break another link in their chains, and to respond with sympathy to their efforts to cope with their difficulties and to realize their own aspirations. Once we relax, some of our blood might move out of our fright glands back into our heart and our head. We might even begin to realize that we can respect people even if we cannot buy them. We might even establish a dialogue with them.

It is often asserted, of course, that we have nothing to learn from the underdeveloped and developing nations. This is an argument based on the assumption that they are obsessed with emulating the United States and other advanced industrial nations, and are thus doing little more than repeating all our mistakes in rapid-fire sequence. Their struggle to escape scarcity is deemed irrelevant to our effort to cope with plenty.

This analysis is relevant only as long as we define our future as a projection of our own past. Only as long, that is, as we do not transcend the limits of our existing marketplace society. But this is precisely what we must do if we are to recognize and overcome the new kind of scarcity we confront as we begin to master the traditional economic scarcity.

We have not transcended scarcity per se. For that matter, we still have many vital decisions — choices — to make concerning how to use the great productive powers we have created. We cannot instantaneously do everything that is possible, let alone everything that will become possible. We have only reached the point where we can begin to deal intelligently and responsibly and democratically with those choices, and the point where we can define the new and different and vastly more difficult kinds of scarcity. This is precisely what Marx was at such pains to point out to us when he argued that capitalism would create the means of conquering economic scarcity, but would not know what to do with that power.

This new kind of scarcity concerns the lack of humaneness and community in relationships between human beings. It is not literally new, of course, but it seems new to us because capitalism defined achievement so narrowly in terms of economic scarcity that we pushed the far more vital issue into the background. Economic success became the definition of life. And it is here, in connection with the scarcity of humaneness in human relationships, in the shortage of community, that the underdeveloped and developing countries can offer us insights and assistance.

They do so merely by existing in their poverty. Once we recognize and accept Marx's point about the scarcity of community under capitalism, for example, we enable ourselves to accept the simple and elementary truth that our existing approach to helping the poor countries perpetuates the scarcity of community. Community is defined by humane human relationships, not by marketplace calculations of profit and loss. Consider Cuba. It tells us that people are still able to commit themselves to the idea and the ideal of the *general* welfare, and to act on that commitment. Cuba tells us that it is better to make a revolution than to give up and accept conditions that offer no serious hope for the future. And Cuba tells us that the humane response to that commitment and that effort is respect, not scorn, and generous help, not embittered and spiteful opposition. And all of these things we need most desperately to relearn.

The poor countries offer us a second kind of assistance because they do have their own traditions and institutions and practices of community. The point is not so much that we should adopt, or even adapt, their particular concepts. That may in some cases be an intelligent approach, but the real help they offer us lies in providing a constant reminder of the idea and the ideal of community. We have so long neglected, and even denied, our own images and practices of community that we need all the encouragement we can find to support our groping efforts to recover and revitalize those traditions.

Other reactions to the validity of Marx's analysis of the capitalist marketplace, and its manifestations in American foreign affairs, lead to dangerous consequences. One such alternative is to define foreign relations in terms of space. This is a continued evasion of the problem, however, because the exploitation and development of space will be conditioned in large measure by events on earth. The other principal approach is to continue the struggle to sustain the existing pattern of capitalist foreign relations. But this offers two equally dismal probabilities. Either the effort will culminate in isolating the United States from a developing world community, or it will eventuate in a nuclear catastrophe.

The cost of continuing the effort to prove Marx wrong is thus exorbitant even by capitalist standards. Indeed, it would seem time to honor the old capitalist axiom of cutting our losses and investing our capital in a more promising venture.

THREE

I*ncreasing Misery and*
Increasing Proletarianization

I. IN THE WORLD MARKETPLACE

> Our sympathy is cold to the
> relation of distant misery
>
> Edward Gibbon,
> *Decline and Fall of the*
> *Roman Empire*

S AVE for a tiny minority, Americans are unanimous in feeling that they have proved Marx wrong about the propensity of capitalism to create increasing proletarianization and increasing misery. Even most habitual radicals declare their fidelity to this American orthodoxy. The consensus is indeed impressive. So, too, is some of the evidence and analysis which supports the doctrine of classless well-being and joy. But there are several significant weaknesses in the argument, and a considerable quantity of contrary facts, which suffice to reopen the issue and to raise major questions as to whether Marx was indeed so simply and totally wrong.

In the first place, the prevailing persuasion is based exclusively on an analysis of the situation in advanced Western capitalist countries. But this involves an abstraction, both from Marx's argument and from reality itself, that is wholly arbitrary and inadmissible in serious evaluation. Marx explicitly and unequivocally grounded his analysis of Western capitalism on the functioning of the world marketplace that it created, which he specified as an inherent structural part of the system. "The real task of bourgeois society is the establishment of the world marketplace. . .and a productive system based on this foundation."

When reviewed within the framework of the world marketplace, as it must be, the evidence concerning misery and proletarianization irrefutably supports Marx.* The colonial or otherwise dependent segment of the capitalist marketplace continues to grow poorer while the Metropolitan sector increases its wealth. Between 1938 and 1958, the share of world income that went to the poor countries dropped from 9 to 6 percent. The United States increased its share by about 6 percent. This is true for the societies which have asserted and won varying degrees of independence but which remain within the capitalist system, as well as for those areas which still exist as formal dependencies. World capitalism has not produced wealth and welfare in its country sector. It has created unemployment, underemployment, and other economic and social and psychological characteristics of misery. This has occurred because the Metropolis has controlled technical progress and other aspects of development in ways

*See P. N. Rosenstein-Rodan, "The International Development of Economically Backward Areas," *International Affairs* (April 1944); H. W. Singer, "Economic Progress in Under-Developed Countries," *Social Research* (March 1949); Gunnar Myrdal, *Rich Lands and Poor* (New York: Harper & Bros., 1957); and K. Buchanan, "Bingo or UNO?" *New Left Review* (October 1963), and the materials cited therein.

detrimental to the weak and poor country sector, and because the inherent imbalance between the two parts of the system has functioned to create such inequality.

It is worth recalling that Adam Smith, the patron saint of capitalism, emphasized this aspect of the system as a fundamental reason for the British to adopt his principles of political economy as high state policy. Smith perfectly understood that the Metropolitan sector of the marketplace enjoyed a structural, as well as simply an initial, advantage over the colonial society. He even argued that this inherent power would enable Great Britain to keep the United States in a dependent role despite its formal political independence.

This skewed, imbalanced, and inequitable relationship is sufficiently dramatic to overcome the normally tranquilizing effect of statistics. Within the capitalist marketplace, the one-sixth of the population in the advanced countries controls and receives about three-fourths of the total wealth of the system. This leaves 48 percent of the people to make do with 8 percent of the income. Perhaps the situation is even more strikingly revealed by realizing that in 1957 – 1958 the terms of trade, which are set by the Metropolis, turned against the poor countries so drastically that they lost more money due to the fall of the prices paid for their products than they received in aid from the advanced countries. Marx has not yet been proved wrong about the increasing misery created by and within the world capitalist system, and since the United States is the dominant Metropolis in that imperium, it cannot be exempted from an evaluation of the results.

An examination of the situation in Latin America is particularly appropriate in this respect. That region has been an integral part of the capitalist marketplace ever since Spain and Portugal conquered it, and the relationship became especially pronounced after those countries lost their economic predominance to Great Britain and the United States. Most of the Latin-American countries still display various elements of a quasi-feudal past, and some of them reveal Indian influences to an even greater degree. The impact of Spanish thought, religion, and custom is likewise manifest. Despite such factors, modern Latin America is nevertheless the product of capitalism operating in the area since the days of the bullionists and the mercantilists. During the last two generations, the United States has moved with increasing vigor to exercise the option on empire that was always inherent in the Monroe Doctrine, and has in the course of that action established a hemispheric informal empire in the region.

The nature of that empire does not disprove either Adam Smith or Karl Marx. Figures for total production in Latin America do show a gross per capita increase of 19 percent in goods and services between 1950 and 1960, but these statistics are unfortunately about as relevant to the true situation as the figure of 61 home runs is to the actual batting skill of Roger Maris. For, despite such gains, the United States continued to grow absolutely and relatively richer than Latin America. In the most favorable part of the decade, across the years 1952–1954, the per capita income of the United States was $1,870. The six highest Latin-American economies ranked in the $250–$499 group, and included Argentina, Chile, Puerto Rico, Cuba, Colombia, and Panama. The remainder of the nations in the area enjoyed per capita incomes of less than $249.

One of the main reasons that the 19 percent increase in total production failed to break the pattern of the rich becoming richer while the poor grew poorer involves the declining rate of growth in Latin America. The growth rate averaged 3.5 percent between 1940 and 1951, and during those years was sufficient to produce a small but steady improvement in most of the countries. At the same time, of course, the United States was gaining even more. But the growth rate began to fall in 1951, and through the next five years slipped to about 2.2 percent. That was not enough to hold the line in the face of population increases. From 1955 to the present, moreover, the rate of growth barely averaged 1 percent, and that signifies a serious absolute, as well as relative, loss of ground. Pain, suffering, death, and social upheavals are the commodities associated with that growth rate.

Another important cause of the crisis is the way Metropolitan capitalism structures the political economy of Latin-American countries in accordance with *its* needs rather than in terms of *their* development. Despite the region's inadequate food supplies (a point dramatized by the reliance of several countries upon imported food even to feed their people as well as they do, and by the general hunger throughout the region), millions of agrarians have been forced or enticed off the land. A few of these people, it is true, actually become property-owning small capitalists. These join their peers in an effective working alliance with more established capitalists, the military, and American interests.

Some of the larger entrepreneurs, who operate primarily as local, national capitalists rather than as associates or agents of American enterprise, do periodically display an inclination to oppose the United States. In a loose, general way, with no exact analogy intended, they can be compared with the wealthy, successful leaders of the American Revolution. "They fear U.S. penetration," one of them recently explained, and worry that "the U.S. is taking over their channels of trade." But their power and independence is limited because they cannot control their own societies without American economic and military aid, and because that assistance can be used against them in their own countries.

The reason for this lies in what happens to the rest of the people who leave the land. Some become workers in the manufacturing and service industries. They want additional benefits, to be sure, but they desire even more strongly to protect the gains they have made. Hence they do not provide a strong, militant base for national capitalism because they associate their improvement with the system dominated by the United States. They are nationalists, of course, but the very effectiveness of the informal empire established by the United States lies in the way their nationalism is channeled into support for local leaders allied with Washington.

Still other Latin Americans who leave the farm move into the white collar bureaucracies—governmental and entrepreneurial—and contribute very little to national development. They function as wage labor of the existing system. They generally identify with it, even when they agitate for pocketbook increases and fringe benefits. The last group, composed of the alienated millions who populate the horrible, miserable slums of the American-built cities, is a threat both to the existing order and to a more national kind of capitalism. The revolution latent in those human beings can in the end be forestalled only if the existing order is modified enough to improve their condition and give them a place in it, or if a strong dynamic national capitalism evolves as an alternative.

If the system established by the United States generated significant and sustained development, or if the national capitalists could obtain enough aid elsewhere to promote the same result, then it is at least conceivable that Latin-American countries could become truly independent capitalist societies. It is highly debatable whether this in itself would solve their major problems, but it would at least offer some grounds on which to challenge the validity of the analyses offered by Adam Smith and Karl Marx. Such has not been the case, however, and it does not seem likely to become so in the visible future.

The current crisis can be dated from the last quarter of 1956. That was when the prices paid for Latin-American products began to fall rapidly below the prices Latin Americans had to pay for their purchases from the United States and other industrial nations. The statistics which define this gap, in terms of the dollar loss involved, sometimes seem to convey the impression that it is a hypothetical matter. In 1959, for example, the decline meant that Latin-American countries received about $1,700 million less for their exports than they would have earned for the same output in 1950. But money that is never received has a way of becoming abstract and ethereal.

The condition becomes very tangible, however, if thought about in terms of the loss of buying power. A Ford tractor cost twenty-two bulls from an Uruguayan ranch in 1954, but required as many as forty-two animals in 1963. It should be realized, furthermore, that the statistics of loss suffered by Latin America represent hard cash that corporations in the United States held in their own bank accounts but did not have to spend on raw materials and other purchases. Hence this seemingly arid data on the terms of trade actually illustrates the pocketbook meaning of the informal empire created by the United States, and demonstrates the essential validity of Marx's analysis of the capitalist world marketplace.

So, too, do the figures on wealth taken out of Latin America by corporations in the United States. In Chile, for example, the corporations earned $77 million in profits in 1959 and sent $71 million to the home office; from Venezuela in 1959 they removed $370 million of $425 million; from Peru in 1960 they remitted $23 million of $26 million; and from Mexico they brought back $77 million of the $96 million earned in 1959 and 1960. In Cuba, investments increased $344 million between 1950 and 1958, but American firms returned $378 million to the United States during the same period. Such amounts of money are apt to be so far beyond the grasp of even we affluent Americans that it may help to translate a unit of $1 million into more familiar commodities. That sum in the United States would feed two adults and five children (including milk) for five thousand months. That is 417 years. Or, to be a bit frivolous, it would buy

143,000 fifths of Old Jack Daniels Black Label sippin' whiskey. Even that figure is somewhat staggering; but if a man sipped a fifth a day, the supply would last him just shy of 400 years.

Such investments by United States firms control 40 percent of the total gross national product of Latin America. That sum is larger than the combined budgets of all Latin-American nations. The overall figures on input and output are equally striking: between 1950 and 1960, for example, United States firms invested $6,179 million in Latin America—but took home $11,083 million. A similar pattern is revealed in the operations of the Inter-American Development Bank.

The Bank is controlled by the United States. All important decisions involving the Ordinary Capital Fund and the Fund for Special Operations are made by two-thirds of the membership. The vote of the United States counts for 41.82 percent of the total. This gives Washington veto power. The third fund, known as the Social Progress Trust or as the Bank of the Alliance for Progress, is controlled by the United States as the supplier of over 90 percent of the money. At the end of the Bank's second year of operation (1962), the United States had contributed $150 million in ordinary capital, compared with $232 million deposited by Latin American nations. While a number of loans had been authorized, less than $70 million had been dispensed.

More money was put to work for Latin Americans in 1963 (the total reached $206 million), but the greatest part of the Bank's funds was serving either the government of the United States or private American financial corporations. The Inter-American Bank received interest on such deposits, of course, but the real gains were made by the private American banks that enjoyed the use of public monies accumulated from taxpayers and deposited with them. Latin Americans were thus contributing to an undramatized and generally unacknowledged Alliance for the Progress of Some United States

Citizens. So, too, of course, were the taxpayers in the United States itself.

Nor should it be thought that such loans are free. They are strictly capitalist operations and for that reason drain even more money from Latin-American economies. If Venezuela is excluded, Latin America uses 13 percent of its foreign earnings from goods and services just to pay current charges on its public loans. If the interest and dividend payments on private investment are added, the total is almost doubled. The figures for the entire world capitalist market-place are comparable. Interest and repayment obligations have the effect of reducing the actual capital secured through new loans and grants to about 70 percent of the gross announced total of such aid.

This essential character of America's informal empire is to some extent mitigated by the modest improvement in a few countries. Puerto Rico, Mexico, Venzuela, and Bolivia are usually mentioned as examples of the positive results of the American system — as was Cuba prior to February 1959. Puerto Rico is generally considered to offer the most striking illustration of such progress; but even in that case the functioning of the informal empire leaves much to be desired — and even expected — if it is judged by its own axioms and claims.*

Most of Puerto Rico's gains have been made since 1945, a period in which the United States increased its aid to the poor countries as part of the Cold War against the Soviet Union. They have appeared, indeed, as part of a general — if implicit — effort by the United States to improve the conditions which reveal that the capitalist system has not disproved Marx's analysis of its general operation. In reality, moreover, Puerto Rico cannot be classed as an independent country,

*The best study of Puerto Rico is by G. K. Lewis, *Puerto Rico: Freedom and Power in the Caribbean* (New York: Monthly Review Press, 1963).

even in a formal sense, and is therefore not typical or representative of the informal empire created by United States capitalism. As the Puerto Ricans themselves point out, the island is, "in effect, an economic region" of the United States and "not a separate economy."

As a consequence, Puerto Rico does not have to bear many of the costs that are essential in an independent nation. The United States pays the full cost of the island's defense, its postal system, its weather bureau, and its consular and diplomatic service. In addition, the United States has given Puerto Rico approximately $500 million since 1898, and is currently providing vast sums to the island. This is massive economic aid. Comparable assistance to other Latin-American countries might well enable them to show similar, if not equivalent, improvement.

But Puerto Rico is not a Latin-American nation. It is essentially a second-class state within the United States, and no Latin-American country would care to pay that price for such help. In this respect, and it is a fundamental one, Puerto Rico should be judged as an American state. Its per capita income, about $700 in the early 1960's, is impressive measured against the poor nations. But it is lower even than the per capita income of Mississippi. And, again like Mississippi, Puerto Rico is not being industrialized in any true sense. A great deal of outside capital has been, and is being, invested to produce items for export and to facilitate the distribution of goods produced elsewhere. This absentee capital controls three of every four factories in Puerto Rico and is handled by non-Puerto Ricans.

The overall impact of America's capitalist system in Puerto Rico was astutely described in the 1960 platform of the island's Popular Democratic party, which never has been a militantly anti-American organization. The party leaders, who have sought, supported, and scrambled for the increasing Americanization of the island, admit that the policy has not created "a good civilization." It has not produced "more tranquility, more serenity, more education, a better civilization, but simply a multiplication of consumer goods, many of them unnecessary." This evaluation can profitably be kept in mind, not only when considering the inherent nature of the informal empire established by the United States in its relationships with Latin-American countries, but also when appraising Marx's judgment of the character of capitalist society per se.

Bolivia's gains are tenuous at best and have been achieved within a framework set and maintained by the United States. The extent and kind of development in Bolivia must be measured against a very striking standard: the country has received from the United States more technical and economic aid per capita than any other country in the world. This assistance began early in the 1940's as part of a complex maneuver to force Bolivia to pay compensation for properties taken from the Standard Oil Company, to block the influence of Argentina, and to prevent Bolivia from making economic deals with Axis powers. The aid was not the product of a general commitment to developing either Bolivia or Latin America. Nor did it produce that result. In 1944, for example, Bolivia was importing about half the food it consumed — most of it from the United States.

The subsequent Bolivian Revolution in 1952 was severely hampered by the consequences of America's earlier informal empire. The revolution nationalized the tin mines, hoping thereby to secure a source of funds for reform and development. But the previous exploitation of the tin reserves by American corporations had so depleted the profitable ores that Bolivia could not compete in the world marketplace where prices were set by the Metropolitan countries. The moderates within the revolutionary coalition turned to the United States for aid and thereby lost a considerable degree of control over the course they could pursue.

Agricultural and manufacturing production have barely held

steady in recent years. The country still imports at least one-third of its food (and continues to obtain it from the United States). All in all, Bolivia provides a clear example of the persuasive power of the United States in Latin America. Its policies and actions contributed significantly to the coming of a revolution. But the same policies left a legacy which drastically limited the revolution's ability to direct the future development of the country. Then, in that context, the United States re-deployed its power and maintained its influence. The case of nearby Chile suggests, however, that such triumphs may not be self-perpetuating. A similar kind and degree of American influence in Chile has been so successful that many observers fear that a Socialist-Communist coalition will sooner, rather than later, win a genuinely free election.

As for Mexico, no one who has even so much as skimmed Oscar Lewis's classic collective biography of *The Children of Sanchez* can ever again be satisfied with gross statistics purporting to show that American operations in that country have been magnificently beneficent. There are more landless peasants than ever before, the oil industry still has not recovered from being owned and exploited by United States corporations, some sections of the country are economically stagnant, if not actually retrogressing, and overall economic development has slowed noticeably since 1957. The educational system is so enfeebled that only 50.7 percent of the 5 – 15 age group is even in school. America has contributed to the improvement of some of Mexico by helping local conservatives transform the nation's once vital revolution into an upper-class reform movement.

The case of Cuba illustrates very clearly the propensity of these Latin-American nations within the informal empire of the United States to stagnate at some point in the process of development as a skewed, imbalanced, and inequitable political economy. (The purchasing power of Cuban exports, for example, was no greater between 1952 and 1956 than it had been between 1932 and 1936.) As they do so, the sequence of events follows very closely the pattern that Marx anticiptated. Severe, sustained social unrest leads either to revolution, to military coups designed to prevent or abort such upheavals, or to action by the Metropolis calculated to reinforce the position of its native allies. Direct military intervention by the United States has not been undertaken during the last generation, but the deployment of armed native forces under the direct and indirect authority of Washington has replaced the older and cruder technique. This is one of the ways in which the United States has institutionalized the structure and strategy of informal empire in a particularly effective manner.

Cuba also dramatizes the way in which this informal empire operates to polarize extremes of wealth and poverty. In the case of Venezuela, for example, the gross statistics of growth are very misleading as to the development of the country. A tiny proportion of the nation's families, 12 percent, holds 50 percent of the gross national income. Such figures indicate why overall increases, actually rather small in any meaningful sense, offer so little improvement to the vast majority. In Colombia, 41 percent of the income is received by 5 percent of the population. The poorest half of the people shares but one-fourth of the total income.

Or, looked at in a different way, one thousand individuals in Argentina control 78 percent of the capital which is worth 90 percent of the gross national product, and they recover 49 percent of the national income. In Guatemala, where the United States has exercised great power and influence over a long period, fifty men control 69 percent of the capital which is valued at 66 percent of the gross national product and earns 50 percent of the national income. And next door in Honduras, a mere twelve men own 90 percent of the capital which returns to them 90 percent of the national income.

Whether considered as a general system, therefore, or evaluated on the basis of the internal patterns of each country, the informal empire established, structured, and sustained by American capitalism has not functioned in a way to disprove Marx. Judged only on the grounds of a raw economic definition of increasing misery and increasing proletarianization, the facts bear out his analysis. The rich are richer and the poor poorer. And the system has generated wide and continuing social unrest culminating in violent revolutions.

When Marx's social and psychological definitions of misery are invoked, his critique is further substantiated. The alienation of millions of human beings — from each other, from their society, and from their own humanness — has been and remains an inherent part of the developmental process involved in the informal empire of the United States. Capitalism asserts and promises that it produces free, creative, and prosperous people through their participation in the competitive marketplace. Yet, even when viewed most generously, the principal product of United States capitalism in Latin America is a class of wage earners who own no entrepreneurial property and hence do not even qualify as first-class citizens within the system. Nor will any significant number of those wage earners ever become entrepreneurs. They begin by being alienated within the system and will remain so alienated.

A vastly greater number of Latin Americans are alienated *from* the system. They exist only and literally outside the society that Metropolitan capitalism has created from part of the population of the region. Capitalism has only increased their misery by deranging and destroying the integrated culture in which they were at least participating members, even if they were poor. The point is not that the traditional society was better per se, or that it should be preserved, but rather that capitalism has not provided either more wealth or more meaning for them. Their misery is to be born and to die as men and women essentially consigned to the limbo between a dying society and a capitalism which denies them first-class citizenship on its terms.

The Alliance for Progress is the overt admission by the United States that Marx's critique of the world capitalist system was essentially correct. It was conceived after the Cuban Revolution to prevent reality from continuing to correspond with Marx's analysis. But there is little if any persuasive evidence that it is designed to strike at the root of the problem, even in capitalist terms, or that it is even functioning to alleviate the crisis in any significant respect. Its object is to make capitalism function faster and better within existing limits, but those limits are themselves the basic cause of the failure.

Truly national and independent capitalist systems in each Latin-American country might prove a viable solution to the region's troubles, at least for an interim period, but no responsible American leader has suggested that the Alliance is attempting to reach that objective. Its purpose is to rationalize and reinforce the established informal empire by improving its poor performance. Among other criteria, economic independence is defined by a multiplicity of relationships. Yet, as policy toward Cuba indicates, the United States was unwilling to allow that nation to break free of the empire even to the extent of making financial transactions with other *capitalist* states. Those same limits have been imposed in other instances. Its own economic difficulties may prevent the United States from making an all-or-nothing effort to block major arrangements of that kind by the large Latin-American countries, but that does not mean the Alliance is conceived as a gracious retreat from empire.

Though the general idea of doing something to improve the functioning of the American informal empire had been discussed periodically ever since the late 1930's, it is quite apparent that Castro's Revolution provoked the first significant action. As originally established, and even as modified, the Alliance is administered within the Organization of American States, whose operation is dominated by the United States. It is clearly designed, furthermore, to help Latin America only within the framework of private investment directed by the United States (and approved associates).

Teodoro Moscoso, who was hand-picked by the United States to run the program, has been commendably candid in describing its broad outlook. "In supporting the Alliance," he remarked reassuringly, "members of the traditional ruling class will have nothing to fear." This was spelled out even more explicitly by Romulo Betancourt, the president of Venezuela, when the program was started, and a man generally praised as the most reliable ally of the United States in all of Latin America. "We must help the poor," he explained, "in order to save the rich." Betancourt was not being carelessly callous when he made that remark. He was simply expressing in straightforward language the central axiom of capitalism which holds that everything depends upon the entrepreneur accumulating large amounts of capital from the operation of the system. Assisting the poor is necessary because capitalism in Latin America has not provided them with enough to sustain the entrepreneur.

In operation, however, the Alliance is not doing very well for either the poor or the rich. Some projects have been successful and some people thereby helped. That is excellent. The trouble is that the vital objective of generating economic development has not even been approached. Felipe Herrera, president of the Inter-American Development Bank, minced no words in discussing this point in November 1963. Not only was Latin America far removed from meeting the minimum necessary growth rate of 2.5 percent, but it was not even maintaining a rate of 1 percent. As a consequence, Herrera warned, there was "a greatly deteriorating situation throughout Latin America." The system is not even functioning as Adam Smith said it should, let alone operating to disprove Karl Marx.

II. AT HOME: ECONOMIC MISERY

*E*very night and every morn
Some to misery are born.

William Blake,
Proverbs, Line 101

WHEN examined in the setting of one national economy within the world capitalist marketplace, and particularly one of the Metropolitan countries, Marx's argument about increasing misery and increasing proletarianization becomes more difficult to evaluate. His analysis was more complicated and detailed, and he was in many respects ambivalent about one of the central points, namely, whether or not such advanced national capitalism could stabilize the system's inherent tendency toward increasing *economic* misery. It may be helpful, therefore, in order to avoid the most common kind of misunderstanding about this involved issue, to emphasize at the outset that Marx did not define *misery* in exclusively economic terms.

His overriding thesis concerned the *condition* of the lower classes, of which money income he considered only one element. "The lot of the laborer, be his payment high or low," Marx commented, "must grow worse." Hence Marx's argument must be evaluated in terms of the social and psychological aspects of misery, and in terms of how and at what costs the economic record itself was made, as well as upon the narrow economic performance measured in dollars and cents.

A discussion of the economic side of the question should begin with a summary of American gains since 1940. During the last two decades, clearly enough, many citizens have benefited from an increase in real income and in the economic standard of living within the United States. This productive triumph merits every word and inflection of the praise Marx offered to such accomplishments by the capitalist system. There is nothing wrong with being better off in the material, economic sense. Indeed, there is a very great deal to be said in behalf of such improvement. Americans should neither find in that achievement, nor manufacture for it, any sense of shame or guilt. Shame and guilt have to do with moral, not economic, considerations.

The recent nature of this economic improvement is very noticeable. People born after 1925 are not much aware of it, but America suffered a severe, wrenching depression between 1929 and 1940. The yearly per capita real income of non-farm employees was only $4 higher in 1934 than it had been in the 1890's. The comparison is particularly relevant, and illuminating, in that both periods were depression eras, and such cyclic behavior is typical of the capitalist system. It also highlights the question of how long economic gains last under American capitalism. These considerations thus serve to emphasize the point that Marx made about the ways in which capitalism generated its economic growth, and the critique he offered of the quality of life it created. Marx was concerned with the costs, the character, the distribution, and the duration of economic benefits, and with the consequences over time of the manner in which they were secured.

His entire analysis was powered by a commitment to the idea and the ideal of all men becoming modern equivalents of classic Greek citizens, and by his awareness of capitalism's failure to realize the individual's potentialities in either the economic or the political or the social realm. Hence a primary aspect of evaluating Marx's critique concerns the social costs of private enterprise capitalism in the United States. The object of discussing economic gains within this context is not to discount or minimize them, but rather to place them in the same framework established by Marx. The real income in dollars received by a man during a portion of his life is only a part of the measure of even his *net* economic position in the system. And it is an even smaller part of what Marx was talking about when he used the word *misery*.

This is of course a broad subject and shades off into the more general question of whether American capitalism has created an ethical and equitable community. Considered in the more narrow economic sense, however, it is clear that the success of the capitalist system is based on large-scale public assistance. American capitalism functions only through the social accumulation of capital, but that capital is not socially allocated. The citizen-contributor does not even do much proposing, and he most certainly does not participate in any significant way in the process of choosing between the alternatives formulated by those who dispose of the capital. American capitalism, and more particularly the entrepreneurial decision-makers of the system, has had its own tax-supported social security plan ever since the Civil War guaranteed it the opportunity and the protection to extend itself over the entire continent and outward into the world marketplace.

The direct and indirect subsidies provided to capitalist entrepreneurs since that time by non-stockholding taxpayers—past, present, and future—defies accurate and final tabulation. The sum is staggering, even if the account is closed after a rough estimate involving the obvious examples of railroads, steamship companies, automobiles, airplanes, the chemical industry, and agriculture. The private use of public monies has been, and continues to be, a central dynamic element in the success of an American capitalism which nevertheless attributes its achievement to the creative powers of private property and individual enterprise. The competitive market economy of capitalism has not been able to sustain itself without continuing and increasing subsidy from the government — meaning the taxpayer.

A more indirect, but by no means less significant, kind of social cost involves the waste, spoilage, misuse, and depletion of the nation's natural resources. This includes human beings as well as other animal and inanimate wealth. The irony here is that the non-stockholding, non-managerial taxpayer must bear not only the wide costs of the initial phases of such misallocation, but is then taxed additionally to support a belated effort to undo the damage and to hold the line against further decimation. One of the few situations in which the public managed some direct, contemporary return on its inherent title to such resources involved the state of Minnesota's tax on the exploitation of its iron ore deposits by private capitalists. The citizens thereby succeeded in diverting some of the profits into the creation of a major university, thus balancing to some extent the depletion of one social resource through the related and partial creation of another. But that example is almost unique, and serves mainly to dramatize the extent to which American capitalism has been financed by social investment of mammoth proportions.

The most disturbing example of these social costs concerns the relationship between war and the success of American capitalism. The issue is not whether capitalism is a unique cause of war. It is not. The causes of war, including the economic ones, operate within capitalism just as they have within other systems of political economy. It does seem demonstrable, however, that capitalism heightens and intensifies the role and impact of economic factors in causing wars. The essential dynamic engine of capitalism, after all, is held to be a never-ending economic competition within a world marketplace.* It further asserts that such rivalry produces health, wealth, and welfare. The argument thus forges a firm, causal bond between victory in the marketplace and other desirable objectives.

This competition has an inherent tendency to escalate into political tension and conflict, and that exacerbates and reinforces other causes of such contention. For this reason, capitalism reveals a strong propensity to produce or result in organized violence. Capitalists may not want war; and, indeed, the business community is always divided at any moment prior to the outbreak of war over whether or not force should be employed. This division arises out of varying estimates by particular interests, and from a similar disagreement among those who take an inclusive view of the system, over whether it is necessary. But the capitalist outlook structures the world in such a way that capitalist leadership often sees itself as being confronted with a choice between war or defeat in the competitive marketplace. War thus becomes the regrettable but necessary means of avoiding failure in the area of human activity previously defined as being crucial to individual and collective achievement.

This does involve an inherent tendency to violence, but it does not supply a unique cause of war. The distinction is crucial, for Marx's analysis of the relationship between capitalism and war is often misread or misinterpreted to an erroneous conclusion. All he actually said was that the capitalist qua capitalist operated according to a set of ideas, and under certain practical necessities, that combined to create a momentum which carried competition over into military combat. And this central proposition is supported by psychological as well as other kinds of evidence.

*See Anatol Rapoport, *Strategy and Conscience* (New York: Harper and Row, 1964).

It is currently fashionable to say that the atom bomb proved Marx wrong in this part of his analysis. The argument unfortunately remains to be demonstrated over a significant period of time. In the first place, the most powerful capitalist Metropolis did use nuclear weapons, and then repeatedly threatened to employ them again. The restraint it has manifested in this area appeared only *after* a state avowing Marxian axioms produced its own nuclear force.* Even if the bomb has the happy result of terminating all-out wars, therefore, it will not have proved Marx wrong. Capitalism can hardly be credited with doing something that it did only in response to being checked by a non-capitalist power.

As for non-nuclear wars, the capitalist world (including the United States) has engaged in a good many such affairs since World War II precisely because it has so narrowly defined the world in the way that Marx said it did. The most striking demonstration of this distortion, which provides more dramatic evidence on this point than even the many colonial wars, involves the way American intelligence operators projected their fears as reality. They grossly miscalculated, misjudged, and overrated Soviet power, and mistakenly assumed that the Soviets would do what a capitalist outlook led them to think the Soviets would do. It seems possible that a different as-

---

*The American proposition for the control of nuclear energy and weapons (generally known as the Baruch Plan) does not contradict this judgment. Under that proposal, for example, the United States declined to specify the circumstances in which it would finally convert its then existing monopoly of nuclear weapons for peaceful uses. It reserved the power to make a wholly unilateral decision on that crucial point. Furthermore, its willingness to share its information and technology for peaceful nuclear development was made contingent upon control of *all* nuclear raw materials in the world, and continuing inspection of the economy of all nations, by a United Nations committee in which it would control a majority vote. Even if it lost there, of course, it could use its veto power in the Security Council to block enforcement of any adverse decision.

sumption concerning Soviet behavior could have been made, even by people not in the slightest contaminated by any serious familiarity with Marx. And, indeed, it was made by a small number of critics, but they were at best ignored or dismissed as dupes or nincompoops, and at worst treated as subversives or even traitors. This suggests that Marx, so far from being wrong, was quite perceptive in his understanding of the way the capitalist defines the world.

These broad aspects of the relationship between capitalism and violence should not divert one's attention from the specific issue of the relationship between war and the domestic economic improvements produced by American capitalism. The point here is that the recent high-level performance which has given rise to the doctrine that America has proved Marx wrong has been achieved only during World War II and the subsequent Cold War with the Soviet Union and the People's Republic of China. The long-range basis of that effectiveness, moreover, was established during the expansion generated by World War I.

It may be true that American capitalism could have produced its recent gains outside the context of war and cold war. But the record shows that the achievement has occurred only during war and cold war, and that evidence cannot be changed or mitigated by a conditional hypothesis. The only way for American capitalism to prove such a claim would be for it to accomplish similar results without war and cold war. It did not do so between 1876 and 1898, between 1900 and 1914, or between 1920 and 1941.

The long depression of the 1870's and 1880's, the panic and depression of the 1890's, the increasingly serious recession of 1913–1914, and the downturn in 1926 which culminated in the Great Depression of 1929–1941, offer persuasive evidence that American capitalism has not been able to accomplish its improvements under the conditions it asserts to be most favorable and most desirable.

Those depressions, to say nothing of other general recessions, or of long-term regional imbalances such as the one between the South and the rest of the nation, represent an incalculable price in human misery — including economic misery — for the overall increase in production and for the short interludes of concentrated general improvement under conditions of peace. At the end of the pre-nuclear period, moreover, American capitalism had simply not created a system that measured up either to its claims or its promises.

Consider, for example, President Franklin Delano Roosevelt's famous warning in 1937 that one-third of the nation was "ill-housed, ill-clad, ill-nourished." Beyond the initial shock it caused, the remark was correctly understood by thoughtful observers to carry a devastating (if unacknowledged) judgment of the functioning of American capitalism, as well as of the effectiveness of the New Deal itself. Even so, the criticism was a model of understatement. The figures Roosevelt used were more than 100 percent optimistic. In 1936, that is to say, 68 percent of the multi-person families of the United States existed under conditions of serious deprivation or outright poverty. That 68 percent of the families received but 35 percent of the nation's family income. This was slightly worse than the situation in 1929, when only 65 percent of the families endured such circumstances.

War and cold war provided the dynamism which enabled American capitalism to improve that performance. The families existing in serious deprivation or poverty dropped to 37 percent by 1947, and to 28 percent by 1963. The major portion of those gains came between the Japanese attack at Pearl Harbor and the termination of the economic war effort. The rate of improvement subsequently slowed very markedly. In his contemporary review of the data, *Rich Man, Poor Man,* Herman P. Miller says without qualification that "there has been no appreciable change in income shares for nearly twenty years." And an even more recent study indicates that the poorest one-fifth of the population received 4.9 percent of total income in 1944, compared with 4.6 percent in 1963.*

For that matter, significant numbers of the poor have become comparatively poorer. "The gap between the earnings of skilled and unskilled," Miller reports, "has widened." The same holds for the Negroes. They gained important ground during the war and by 1947 were earning roughly 50 percent as much as the whites. In all but two states, however, they lost ground between 1949 and 1959. The general division of income looked like this in 1959:

The *bottom* 13 percent of families received 2 percent of total income;

The *top* 15 percent of families received 37 percent of total income;

The *bottom* 40 percent of families received 17 percent of total income;

The *top* 40 percent of families received 67 percent of total income; and

The *bottom* 54 percent of families received 28 percent of total income.

The people in the lower half of the system have clearly benefited from the increase in total production since 1941, and hence their low relative position does not represent an across-the-board absolute decline. But Marx was primarily and explicitly concerned with the *condition* of such employees, whatever the level of their wages or income; and their relative income position does bear on their condition, as do even more the circumstances surrounding their betterment, and the nature and tone of the society created by the means used to accomplish such improvement.

---

*See J. M. Fitzwilliams, "Size Distribution of Income in 1963," *Survey of Current Business* (April 1964).

The same-sized slice of a bigger pie does provide the wage earner with more pie. So, up to a point, does a slightly smaller slice of a bigger pie. But that approach to the question of the condition of the worker begs many of the central issues. It is like saying that having a television set compensates for the lack of modern plumbing and running water in the house. It may, but only if one has accepted a value system that ranks television ahead of sanitation. This attitude ignores the non-economic prices the worker has to pay for the same slice of pie, and the total cost to him of the way it is produced. And the last of these considerations, including as it does the subsidies he provides the system, clearly decreases his net economic share of the general improvement. American capitalism can hardly substantiate its claim to have proved Marx wrong simply because it manages to camouflage its inability to function according to its own axioms. That is success of a kind, to be sure, but it is not of an order sufficient to meet the real issue.

As for non-economic costs, the role of military activities in the overall achievement of American capitalism should be apparent in connection with the years of preparation for and engagement in sustained violence between 1940 and 1945. Today, in the 1960's, economic activity directly connected with the military accounts for 10 percent of the gross national product. This includes, for example, 20 percent of the income of the manufacturing industry, about 50 percent of total production in the electrical industry, and over 60 percent of the work in the shipbuilding sector. Such specifically and directly military employment accounts for 11 percent of the total labor force.

This share, which involves at least 33 percent of American scientists and engineers (and 48 percent of all American research), does not include the men who are employed in the armed forces per se. This military pay roll is twice as large as the auto industry's, and one and a half times that of the iron and steel industry. Even when computed with a bias toward underestimation, this direct and indirect military employment accounts for about 20 percent of the total labor force. This figure, which does not include the men who are employed in what passes for the civilian sector of the economy in a cold war environment, comes within 5 percent of the maximum estimates of unemployment in 1933.

Despite this assistance from the military sector, and with the further help provided by the non-military aid programs likewise financed by the taxpayer, American capitalism still has not reduced economic misery to minor levels. Today, in 1964, between 35 and 50 million Americans exist in severe deprivation or outright poverty. There is substantial and persistent unemployment in twenty major industrial communities and in ninety other regional areas. And there are still ten million housing units lacking electricity, running water, and sanitary facilities.

One of the reasons that so much stress is placed on having proved Marx wrong is that a discussion pointed in that direction serves—intentionally or otherwise—to distract attention from such appalling failures of capitalism. Even if Marx is read to the unequivocal conclusion that, over the long haul, economic misery would increase under capitalism (and that interpretation is not at all the obvious matter it is made out to be), the record does not justify any flat assertion that he was wrong. Surely a system cannot be judged a success if it performs well only under conditions of war and extreme international tension, when its claims are so vastly different. Or, further, when its standard of success discounts poverty and suffering of such broad dimensions as incidental.

To approach the issue in a different way, consider the more narrowly economic record. The Spanish-American War played a significant role in sustaining and enlarging recovery from the grave economic crisis of the 1890's, which itself came at the end of a long cycle of recessions and depressions. World War I then pulled the American economy out of a major recession in 1913–1914 that revealed most if not all of the indications of becoming a serious depression. Those two wars enabled the economy to function without such a relapse for a period of roughly thirty years. (To be more than generous, the serious post-war depression of 1920–1922 has been discounted.) On this basis, with World War II and the Cold War considered as being similar in their effects to the role of the earlier conflicts, there is little justification for assuming that American capitalism has reached—let alone transcended—its next major crisis. An economic crisis, that is, which evolves in a period of relative international calm and which is not solved and overcome through the effects of international crisis and conflict.

American capitalism has never since 1861 functioned effectively enough to decrease economic misery over any significant period of time, save as it has been stimulated by war or cold war.

For that matter, the system is not presently functioning even as well as it did a few years ago. In one central area, that of creating new capitalists, it is not performing with any notable or striking success. Of the spending units in the nation in 1960, 24 percent had no liquid capital; another 21 percent had less than $200; and a total of 63 percent had less than $1,000. These figures may be less startling when it is realized that the lowest 30 percent of income earners failed to increase their 9 percent share of total income between 1950 and 1959. And while average weekly earnings increased 45 percent between 1939 and 1945, the rate of improvement dropped by almost two-thirds, to 16 percent, between 1945 and 1959. For that matter, weekly earnings did not return to the 1945 level until mid-1952, well after the Korean War had started.

Clearly enough, moreover, the system is creating far more wage earners than capitalists. New capitalists do enter the marketplace. But only a few manage to survive, and only an infinitesimal number of those ever exercise any significant influence in the marketplace. Between 1950 and 1960, for example, 82 percent of all new businesses failed, and in manufacturing the death rate was 91 percent. The decline in the number of farm owners and farm workers is better known, if only because the taxpayer has been called upon to provide subsidies for those who remain and welfare assistance for many of those who were forced to abandon agriculture.

The issue is not the welfare payments per se. Those are wholly justified and should be broadened in intent and scope, as well as in amount. The real point concerns the inability of American capitalism to function without such subsidies. If this is what is meant when it is said that Marx has been proved wrong by the internal transformation of capitalism, then it should be apparent that the issue is being misunderstood, begged, or simply obscured. The system can hardly be judged a success simply on the performance of a drastically decreasing number of capitalists. This standard neglects the subsidies they receive and ignores all those who have ceased to be capitalists by being transformed into wage earners.

And it is by no means clear that the system is functioning even under the stimulus of the Cold War in a way that will sustain the performance of the years between 1940 and 1949. Each recession since the Korean War has left more men and women without jobs, and the resulting lack of work is beginning to create a permanent class of unemployed. American capitalism is simply not creating enough new jobs. Between 1953 and 1963, for example, the manufacturing industry failed to add a single *net* job. In transportation, not a single net job has been provided since 1929. Nothing really dramatizes the extent to which American capitalism relies and depends upon the taxpayer as effectively as the fact that government created more than half the new jobs that appeared between 1960 and 1963. Private enterprise provided 76 percent of the job growth between 1947 and 1957, but since then the government has supplied 64 percent of new employment.

There has been a 20 percent drop in unskilled jobs between 1950 and 1960. Unemployment among such men and women, which had dropped from 30 percent in 1940 to 12 percent in 1950, had by 1961 begun moving back (passing 20 percent) toward the depression figures. The same cycle appeared in the semi-skilled and skilled sectors of the labor market. In 1940, for example, 13 percent of the semi-skilled workers were unemployed, whereas only 6 percent were out of work in 1950; but the total was back to 12 percent in 1961. The statistics for unemployed skilled workers were 15, 6, and 10 percent for the same years.

Even more critical, at least in many respects, is the inability of the system to re-integrate such men into the marketplace. They remain out of work longer, and they tend to go back to work—when they find it—at lower incomes. Even as early as the years 1947–1948, when the economy was stimulated by postwar consumer, military, and aid expenditures, 51 percent of the people in low income groups stayed in that bracket. Those who climbed significantly (a mere 4 percent) were balanced by others (5 percent) who fell by the same amount. Only those who climbed a small amount, into the $2,000 per year bracket, outnumbered those who fell back into the $1,000 group.

Ten years later, in 1958, 30 percent of *all* men employed had earned less than $3,000 in 1957; and of the men unemployed in 1958, 38 percent had earned less than $2,000 and 56 percent had received less than $3,000. Of all the people unemployed in 1962, 25 percent of them had been out of work for more than six months in 1961. And the 9.6 million who had been unemployed for one month or longer in

1961 had an average income of a meager $2,300. By 1963, the men and women who had been without jobs between fifteen and twenty-six weeks accounted for 12.8 percent of the total, and those unemployed more than half a year came to 13.5 percent.

It should not be surprising, therefore, to learn that public assistance expenditures almost doubled between 1953 and the end of 1963, or that the total number dependent on such help is now over seven million. One type of such assistance, aid to dependent children, jumped almost threefold across the years of war and cold war. A particularly hard-hit area like Pulaski County in southern Illinois offers an excellent picture of what all this means in an established community. During the 1950 – 1960 decade, population declined 23 percent while public welfare costs increased 66 percent. Today, in 1963, one of every five remaining residents is on relief. A similar situation exists in Clay County, Kentucky, where 50 percent of the families have incomes of less than $1,800, and 70 percent receive less than $3,000. Fourteen percent of the families receive welfare payments.

The Negro, of course, is at least twice as bad off as the white man. That, for example, is a recent comparative statistic on adult Negro unemployment. In any full accounting, however, it is simply impossible to quantify either the nature or the extent of the Negro's inferior position. This massive failure of American capitalism can only be approached and comprehended as a central part of its more general inability to create and sustain a moral and equitable community through the operation of the marketplace.

In a similar way, the nature of the emancipation that women have sought and won within American capitalism is more aptly discussed within the broader context. But economic data does serve to characterize one aspect of their successful struggle to enter the marketplace. The number of family units increased by 11.3 percent, for example, between 1950 and 1958, but the number of those units headed by women jumped almost twice that amount. This might appear to be full emancipation in the vein of Winnie the Breadwinner, until it is noted that the percentage of women involved either as individuals or as heads of families in the lowest one-fifth of income earners also rose steadily. It was 20 percent in 1939, 30 percent in 1947, and 35 percent in 1956. It may at least be questioned whether the psychic wealth of emancipation, particularly when it is achieved within a negative psychological framework, is sufficient to counterbalance such economic difficulties. Women are also a significant economic group further along up the income ladder. Their labor is necessary in more than 65 percent of the families that manage to accumulate an income of $10,000 or more a year.

Working women, single or married, impose an additional burden on an economy already having great difficulty in maintaining its recent gains against deprivation and poverty. This is not an oblique way of saying that females should stay at home confined to the bed, the sink, and the washing machine, although the present situation does suggest that the definition and content of emancipation might somehow be broadened to include something beyond the competitive rivalry of the marketplace. The principal issue in this context has been stated very clearly by a member of the Department of Labor. "The economy will have trouble enough in the years ahead just providing jobs for the increasing working-age population. With a larger proportion of adults seeking jobs, on top of the inevitable population rise, I can't see anywhere for unemployment to go but up."

Three times as many jobs will have to be created during the remainder of the 1960's as appeared between 1957 and 1963 if unemployment is to be stabilized at its present level. This will be a staggering task even if the circumstances remain static. The crude unemployment statistics that are usually cited in newspapers and magazines do not indicate the full extent of the problem. "Approximately 14 million men and women," explained Secretary of Labor W. Willard Wirtz, "were unemployed at some time during the year 1962. . . .Unemployment is affecting a very large number of people, almost one-fifth of the work force. . . [and] is becoming an all-too-permanent condition for a 'hard core' group of men and women." Yet, to make any substantial headway against this situation, the economy needs to provide eighty thousand new jobs a *week*. That amounts to creating a new General Motors Corporation payroll every seven days for at least a decade.

The more accurate estimates of total unemployment in August 1963 varied between 6.8 and 7.4 percent.* The percentage figure is apt to be very misleading: the extent of unemployment is more fully appreciated if it is discussed as affecting six million human beings in the direct, immediate sense. Even that is somewhat vague and beyond easy comprehension. Hence it may help to visualize the entire labor force of Illinois, the fourth most populous state in the union, as being out of work. In this way, among other things, one gains a sense of how many other people are directly and indirectly affected — psychologically and socially, as well as economically — by the unemployment of one man.

The same point can be grasped by realizing that the entire family and marriage structure within various communities in West Virginia and Kentucky has been warped and wrenched into new and by no means constructive forms as a result of such concentrated unemploy-

*As with other statistics cited throughout, this unemployment figure fluctuates from month to month. The range of such changes, and in particular the extent of periodic decreases, is not, however, sufficient to disprove the broad analysis of the system. It is perhaps wise to make the same point in connection with the periodic and dramatic announcements of a new loan to some poor or developing country. Such grants do not change the fundamental relationship between the U.S. and such countries.

ment. Given the nature of the national mania about female emancipation, it is difficult to discuss such matters candidly without being accused of making remarks against the freedom of women. The popularity of the subject, and the dreary and unrelieved seriousness with which it is treated, has the effect of leading people to forget that there are other ways of being emancipated than simply entering the competitive marketplace in the image of a male.

Let it be agreed, therefore, that both society and the individual can benefit from changes in the role and activities of women. But to make such changes after rigorous thought and with a willingness to introduce further modifications if the first ones have negative consequences is quite different from the inclination to accept and even applaud changes that occur quite incidentally, and which bear only superficial similarities to the avowed and desired objective.

The events in West Virginia and Kentucky are of the second variety. They have been caused by the malfunctioning of American capitalism, and the female emancipation involved is a rather grisly affair. As the men lose their jobs, the women go to work in the textile mills that have moved into the areas to take advantage of the new labor pool. But more than work is involved, for the whole structure of individual, family, and social roles is changed: the women try to adapt to the outlook and the working day of the male, while the men struggle to function within the female framework.

The impact and consequences of the first phase, unemployment, are succinctly summarized in a report on a similar area in Minnesota. "The stress of unemployment tends to separate rather than to mold the family into a smoother functioning unit. . . .There seems to be an increase in the hostile reaction toward one another and also toward society. . .the wife blames the husband for being out of work. . . .In many instances the roles become reversed. In many of these situations, the family is never able fully to recover."

A West Virginia woman has provided direct comment on the specific situation in her region. "Here we have strong men proud of their families, proud of their abilities to support their families, thrown out of work. A man looks for a job and finds none. His unemployment compensation expires. His wife goes to work, and he stays home and looks after the children.

"What happens to that man? What happens to that home? In many cases, he loses his self-respect. He becomes demoralized, and the family is broken up."

Sometimes the man destroys himself. A Kentucky newspaperman told the following story about one of his friends. The man had been unemployed for three years despite vigorous and extensive efforts to find a job. His wife's income barely kept the family from starvation and the elements. The man finally concluded that his death benefits were the only contribution he could make to the welfare of his family. "So," the newspaperman explained, "as a Christmas present to his wife and his eight children, the man took out his shotgun and calmly killed himself. It was the best Christmas present he knew how to give. Living he was of no help to his family. By dying he could feed them."

The children also suffer. In doing so, they add their own particularly intense commentary on the disruption of family roles and relationships. Here is the way it affected the two-year-old daughter of a skilled worker in Indiana. Her father had been out of work for thirteen months. "She began to have nightmares," the father explained. "She tended to be disobedient and just completely frustrated and to just be honest, she just didn't know who was mama around the house."

No one really knows what the social and personal consequences will be if the process continues indefinitely, but so far it has caused great pain and suffering. If it be said that this is not true emancipation, then the whole issue of emancipating the men along with the women is raised in an inescapable way. After all, the work routine of West Virginia miners has structured their existence for generations. But the main point in this specific discussion involves the involuntary nature of the entire process. The people concerned did not decide to try a reversal of roles on lower incomes as an experiment in better living. It was imposed upon them by the failure of the impersonal marketplace of American capitalism to function according to its axioms and its claims.

The West Virginia situation also illustrates an even more fundamental aspect of the contemporary performance of American capitalism. On the one hand, there is the issue of sophisticated mechanization, technological substitutes for old materials, and the depletion of resources. These considerations raise serious problems in their own right. But the second difficulty is automation, and its mature form of cybernated production. Once these factors are introduced into the capitalist political economy, Marx's reference to the growing number of men whose "specialized skill is rendered worthless by new methods of production" takes on all the relevance of a contemporary monograph by a card-carrying industrial sociologist. Indeed, the November 1962 issue of the *Monthly Economic Letter,* published by the First National City Bank of New York, might understandably be confused with a comment by Marx himself on the same subject. "Automation represents the quintessence of capitalism," the bank explained, "the ultimate in the investment of money to get the biggest product out of human labor."

The bank was accurate. Cybernated production is the crowning achievement of the competitive capitalist marketplace. Men have been so incited, organized, and directed that they have finally produced machines that replace men in the fundamental sense. All mechanization has relieved men of labor, of course, but recent and contemporary advances go far beyond this traditional kind of assistance and its associated temporary unemployment. On the one hand, some machine systems, which do not really qualify as cybernated production units, do so much work in such a short period of time that they destroy so many jobs so quickly and permanently that the entire industry (and, often, the entire area) is structurally changed in a drastic manner. The men and women who have been replaced by the machines have not been re-absorbed into *any* existing sector of the marketplace. Nor is there any reason to believe that the capitalist system, functioning according to its own anxioms, will ever re-employ them.

True cybernated production goes much further. It creates a system that can in many respects — and they are very many, indeed — control itself. A cybernated production line not only changes products automatically, but it can correct its own errors. Some can even repair themselves. This not only displaces still more men and women, but it increases the requirements for those few who are still needed. They have to be better educated, more thoroughly and carefully trained, and particularly responsible. The elements in such a cybernated production line, furthermore, can themselves be made in a cybernated factory. Hence the displacement of people begins to accelerate once cybernation is introduced in complementary sectors of an industry — or of the economy itself.

From the point of view of the capitalist, therefore, cybernation offers a way to reduce labor costs, to rationalize the human beings who remain, and to free the corporation from countless earlier restrictions connected with such problems as plant location and product distribution. Bankers estimate that cybernation threatens approximately 20 percent of their employees. To be sure, the banking business is growing and will therefore create more jobs in the coming years; but it cannot be counted on to produce as many jobs as it would have prior to cybernation. In one case, for example, a bank cut the number of its bookkeepers by 80 percent over a period of four years. Some of them, but only some of them, were retained in other capacities. Another bank displaced all its bookkeepers and was able to find new tasks for half of them. These figures serve to dramatize the general situation. Unemployment among clerical workers rose from 2.8 percent in January 1957 to 4.6 percent in January 1962. Cybernation replaces brains as mechanization replaces muscles.

American agriculture has been undergoing similar and drastic changes even without true cybernation, and hence offers a good example of the nature and extent of the restructuring that is involved in such developments. One expert recently described the process as it affected one phase of farming in the following way: "Modern vegetable farms with irrigation have become a controlled manufacturing process. . .and should be considered as such in legislation." The result certainly does not disprove Marx's analysis of the central tendency of capitalism to centralize, consolidate, and accentuate the extremes of wealth — while all the time driving the weaker entrepreneurs on toward the edges and then ultimately out of the marketplace. Of the 6.8 million farms which existed in 1935, only 3.7 million remained in 1962, and the number will very probably drop to 1 million within fifteen years. One of the main reasons for this is simply that more and more people lack the capital to remain farmers. Investment per worker on competitive farms averaged \$21,300 in 1960, as compared with \$15,900 in other industries.

The rich farms have been getting richer and the poor farms have been disappearing from the face of the land. Farmers owning a thousand or more acres controlled 28 percent of all agricultural property in 1962. A mere 3.7 percent of the farmers owned 49 percent of the land. The very top farmers, who comprise 3 percent of the industry, produce more than the bottom 78 percent. Their share of total production jumped from 50.7 percent in 1950 to 71.7 percent in 1959. At the bottom of the statistical hill reside 1.6 million farmers, 44 percent of all the industry.

Within that group, moreover, there are 350,000 families whose income from agriculture is $438 per year. They manage to add $525 from all other sources for a grand total income of $963 per year. Another 1.3 million units are sliding into the puddle at the bottom, and their momentum will very probably drown them. They already earn a bit more away from the farm ($1,816) than they do on it ($1,740), and their share of farm sales dropped from 37 percent in 1950 to 23 percent in 1959.

Many of the smaller and middle-sized operators who manage to survive in any form will undoubtedly do so by becoming absorbed into contract, wage-labor farming. This turning of the old entrepreneurial farmer into a wage earner is far along in the poultry industry, and is also established in pork, beef, and milk. Assembly-line agriculture is integrated under the control of large corporate enterprises from the production, storage, and milling of grain, through hatcheries and processing plants, to packaging and merchandizing the birds in chain stores. A typical chicken factory, though by no means one of the largest, turns out 9,600 birds per hour.

The ironies in this agricultural situation come almost as fast as the birds in the broiler plant. The consumer who has a job can of course buy more of this food with the same amount of labor than he did in 1939. This is all to the good. But the cost cannot really be reckoned simply in terms of the over-the-counter price. The consumers also paid a total of $22.1 billion in subsidies to agriculture between 1952 and 1961. Net farm income in 1961 was $12.9 billion, for example, but $5.9 billion came from the taxpayer. His share for 1962 increased to $7.2 billion. Most of this money went to large landowners and primarily helped the rich become richer.

It is more difficult to put a price tag on the human suffering involved in this process. Without any doubt, however, President Kennedy was correct in concluding that unemployment "wastes the lives of men and women." Some of the costs are paid by the children of migratory farm workers in the form of poor education which short-circuits their future. Other dues are collected from the emotions and the bodies of the people who are driven off the land. But neither the psychologists nor the sociologists have yet agreed upon a formula for converting these losses into dollars and cents.

Other sectors of the economy offer equally striking examples of how advanced mechanization and cybernation not only extract "the biggest product out of human labor" on the job, but also how they drastically reduce the amount of labor required for the job. It is true that manufacturing employment rose 12.8 percent across the years 1947 – 1952, as production jumped 39.4 percent. Those figures, however, indicate that the machines were elbowing the men away from the pay window. And between 1952 and 1961, when production went up 17.4 percent, employment in production jobs went down by 5.8 percent. The rate may even be increasing: a Department of Labor study of two hundred manufacturing plants between 1957 and 1961 revealed a production increase per man-hour of 17.7 percent and a decrease in employment of 8.4 percent. To visualize the results in a different way, consider that 1.5 million production jobs simply disappeared between 1955 and 1963. Such results were not yet so obvious in the service industries, but the trend was well established. In New York City alone, for example, programmed systems have replaced forty thousand elevator operators in the last five years. And the unemployment rate for non-household service workers in 1963 reached 6.3 percent.

Such talk about cybernation destroying jobs is very apt to strike the average citizen like overhearing a story about a fire involving a man in a different state told by a man he happened to be standing next to on a bus who had himself read about it in a newspaper. This is not the case. "You can talk all you want to about automation being the harmless successor to the Industrial Revolution," remarked one Midwestern labor leader in a city of 150,000, "[and] the easy retraining of employees to better jobs, and the better life to come. But this is today, and here's a human being, with kids in school and a mortgage on his house, and there's nothing else that he can do."

Mechanical tree-shakers, for example, do the work of eighty men and women. Fourteen people controlling fourteen machines can produce 90 percent of all the light bulbs used in the United States. Two men can produce a thousand radios per day; it used to require two hundred men to make that many. And an insurance company, by installing automatic equipment in only *one of its sections*, cut employment from 198 to 85, *and reduced its equipment cost from $235,000 to $19,000*. But these small and random illustrations do not fully reveal the fundamental impact of cybernation throughout an entire industry, and that is where the structural changes are being made.

In the chemical industry, for example, production increased 27 percent between 1955 and 1962 while production jobs decreased by 3 percent. In the thirteen years after 1947, textile production held constant while employment dropped about 40 percent. Or, to visualize the impact of cybernation in a different way, consider that it enabled the Jones and Laughlin Steel Company to boost its earnings 11 percent in 1961 while producing less and selling less. A similar pattern evolved at the Buick plant in Flint, Michigan. By the end of 1962, it was employing only half the number of workers to produce the same number of cars as it had manufactured approximately five years earlier.

The electrical industry, meanwhile, increased production 20

percent across 1953 – 1959 while reducing production employment by 10 percent. During just half that time (1956 – 1959), the single firm of General Electric increased output 8 percent even though it cut its worker payroll by 25 percent. And, during the decade 1952 – 1962, Bell Telephone handled a 50 percent higher load of calls with only 10 percent more personnel. But the stark drama of cybernated production is probably best revealed in three further illustrations. One involves a plant recently constructed by Continental Copper and Steel Industries. Its new $3 million copper rolling mill requires three men per eight-hour shift. One engineer sets the controls, and two other men load the conveyors and then unload the finished rods. Among other things, this example indicates why labor unions are deeply concerned lest cybernated production subvert their financial position as well as shorten their membership lists.

The second case study does not even embody full cybernation, although it does include a good deal of automatic equipment. The shift from steam locomotives to diesel engines took place in the short period between 1947 (14.6 percent diesel) and 1960 (97 percent diesel). This change-over resulted in the following *decrease* in railroad personnel:

Equipment Maintenance	50 percent
Right-of-Way and Structures	55 percent
Clerical	31 percent
Miscellaneous	27 percent
Executives	1 percent

The third instance concerns a conversation between Walter Reuther, head of the United Auto Workers and Vice President of the AFL – CIO, and the president of a corporation making cybernated equipment. The subject, not surprisingly, was whether or not cybernation was creating enough jobs to offset those it destroyed. The president remarked that his firm expected to double its output over the next five years, but then added that "we are going to have to break our neck trying to keep as many employees as we have now." The meaning is implicit but nevertheless clear: cybernated equipment and systems are even now beginning to be produced by cybernated assembly lines. The machines are replacing the men in the making of the machines that replace still other men.

Considered in the light of these facts, instead of through the distorting lens of anti-Marxist ideology, cybernated production raises substantial doubts as to whether Marx was indeed so very wide of the mark. His argument had three parts, and it is now useful to recapitulate each one in relation to the others. The first held that the inherent logic of the capitalist system pushed it toward creating increasing economic misery for an increasing number of people. The second explicitly noted the existence and operation of several factors which counter-balanced and delayed the realization of that dreary and intrinsic nature. The third involved his estimate of the outcome of the clash between those conflicting forces within the system.

At various points in his work, Marx concluded that the drift of the system toward increasing misery would very probably prove decisive. In his later years, however, he acknowledged the possibility that the tendency to misery could be slowed down indefinitely by a combination of the opposing factors, and that the transition to socialism could occur without the kind of violent mass revolution that he had earlier anticipated erupting in the last phases of increasing misery.

A serious evaluation of Marx's position on the basis of the American evidence has to come to terms with each of these parts of his argument. The power and validity of the first section of his analysis is undeniable. American capitalism has regularly stumbled into panics, recessions, and depressions. It has consistently produced a society characterized by extremes of wealth and poverty, and power and impotence. The system has routinely driven the entrepreneur into the role of wage laborer, who thereafter scrambles to hold his position against the pressures which threaten to reduce his well-being even further. And both in its performance as the Metropolis of a vast informal American empire and as the leader of the world's Metropolitan powers since 1941, it has not disproved Marx's argument about the actual performance of the world capitalist marketplace.

The American record likewise verifies the second part of Marx's analysis. In all probability, American capitalism offers the classic illustration of the counterbalancing forces that Marx identified. The United States has in effect been an empire unto itself in terms of resources. Combined with that wealth, its growing population served for more than a century the imperial function that Adam Smith described, and thereby provided a wholly controlled and expanding marketplace. Its great relative security and open political system gave the entrepreneur a grandiose freedom to operate as a capitalist. The same considerations encouraged the untrammeled application of technological advances. The Negro provided a major pool of depressed labor throughout the history of the system; and other Americans and immigrants periodically swelled that reservoir to even greater proportions. And its foreign trade, first in cotton, then in food stuffs, and finally in manufactured goods, also made a significant contribution to the system's development and its ability to sustain itself against the forces of collapse.

The strength of these countervailing factors is the basis of the argument that American capitalism also proved Marx wrong on whether or not the system would be able to overcome its inherent tendency toward increasing economic misery. To be taken seriously, however, this critique of Marx must acknowledge that subsidies from taxpayers, wars, and cold wars have played a central causative role in forestalling such misery. We can rejoice over the wealth, but we might profitably ponder whether or not the many unrecognized and hidden costs embodied in those gains, and the resulting contemporary system of private control over social production, actually add up to a persuasive defense of capitalism.

There remains, moreover, the crucial question of whether or not American capitalism will actually hold the gains of the period since 1941. It is by no means clear that it will be able to accomplish that task. Cybernated production combined with capitalist principles of political economy may indeed produce increasing unemployment and decreasing income for an increasing number of families and individuals. At the moment, therefore, the most that can be said is that twenty years of war and cold war, and increasing public subsidies, enabled American capitalism to extricate itself from the Great Depression and produce additional wealth for approximately half the population.

After all, Marx has to be judged on the long-term performance of capitalism, not on a short period selected after the fact. There is an illuminating, if also sobering, aspect of all the outpouring of self-congratulation that has occurred during the last fifteen years. The same people who are now dancing on the grave of Marx were equally distraught between 1943 and 1947 over what they expected to be a renewal of the Great Depression. They are now apparently satisfied to preserve the ideology and the private control of social resources that characterize modern American capitalism, and the material gains of the period, even at the cost that has been paid for that accomplishment. Before agreeing with and accepting that judgment, however, it seems wise to consider other entries on the bill.

III. AT HOME: MISERY AS ALIENATION

> *Apothecary.* My poverty, but not my
> will, consents.
>
> *Romeo.* I pay thy poverty, and
> not thy will.
>
> William Shakespeare,
> *Romeo and Juliet,* Act V

CYBERNATED production also serves to dramatize the other—the non-economic—side of the increasing misery that Marx associated with the capitalist system. When Marx talked about misery ultimately producing revolution, he by no means confined his argument to the proposition that revolution depended *solely* upon increasing economic misery. He was far too sophisticated a student of human history and human psychology to commit that reductionist fallacy. The additional, and equally important, feature of misery concerned the alienation of man—socially from other men, individually from himself, and historically from his own true nature. It is often maintained that Marx de-emphasized this aspect of misery in his later years. The argument holds that his concern with such physiological and psychological factors was merely a part of his youthful philosophical and romantic radicalism, and that it disappeared after he turned to study the economic and political facets of the capitalist system. This is not true. But, even if it were, it could not therefore be excluded from his general critique — or bypassed in any serious evaluation of his argument.

Marx never dismissed alienation as an inherent part of capitalism and the human misery that it produced. He did not even totally abandon the word "alienation." What he did do, as in the three volumes of *Capital*, was to shift to three synonyms. One of these, "dehumanization," is in some respects more explicit and evocative than the term "alienation" itself. The others, "the fetishism of production," and the "fetishism of commodities," may jar the ear, and also qualify as jargon typifying the self-consciousness of modern economists and sociologists. Granting those objections (which have some merit), it still remains true that Marx used the phrases to characterize the alienation inherent in capitalism. It can even be argued that his introduction of the concept *fetish* reveals an increasing insight into the psychology of the possessive individualism upon which capitalism rests. The suggestion that many people develop an unreasoning devotion to production per se, and to an interminable acquisition of things which are believed to carry the magic power to solve all social and individual problems, does enlarge one's understanding of capitalist society.

Marx concluded that alienation was caused by several interrelated aspects of capitalism. One was the outgrowth of the progressive use of machinery within capitalist assumptions. Alienation did not result from machinery qua machinery, but rather from machinery which was beyond the ability or power of individuals or small groups to acquire and adapt to their own entrepreneurial and creative activity. A lathe, for example, does not in and of itself alienate a man. But a lathe used within limits wholly set by other men, and for only the repetitive performance of one of its many functions (as, say, for the endless production of one inch wood screws), can lead to alienation.

A second and related development occurred as part of the increasing exclusion of an increasing number of men from any participating role in the system. The successful functioning of capitalism destroyed more and more of its protagonists. The system not only alienated capitalists from the means of production, but further alienated men as workers because the machinery as employed and organized destroyed any creative relationship to the work itself. As this happened, men began to be divorced from their own historical nature. They ceased to view themselves, even ideally, as creatures in the tradition of the Greek citizen or the Renaissance man. This meant that the very conception of possible achievement had been drastically and dangerously reduced. *Men began to settle for less in their very definition of Man.*

More and more capitalists thus became mere attendants to machines over which they exercised no significant control. Under capitalism, Marx argued, "the instruments of labor, when they assume the form of machinery, acquire a kind of material existence which involves the replacement of human force. . .in which the worker is nothing more than an appendage to the extant material conditions of production." The result, he concluded, was "that the work is *external* to the worker, that it is not a part of his nature, that consequently he does not fulfill himself in his work but denies himself, has a feeling of misery, not of well-being. . . .[The work] is not the satisfaction of a need, but only a *means* for satisfying other needs."

Marx was not saying that the other needs were marginal or unworthy, but rather that the act of work had been devalued and dehumanized, and rendered uncreative, and further torn out of any direct relationship with the satisfaction of other human needs. "The more the worker produces. . .the more value he creates," Marx explained; "the less value — the less dignity — he himself has." Money became the symbol of this entire process. It was the token "of man's work and existence, alienated from man," which dominates him. "Making things saleable," Marx concluded, "is the practical side of alienation."

Such dehumanization of work, and unemployment per se, provide the most obvious illustrations of alienation. Within the capitalist framework, at any rate, productive work within the marketplace arena provides the foundation of an individual's sense of value, and hence of his dignity. By definition, as well as in daily experience, a man outside the marketplace is a non-functioning element in the system. Neither casual disparagements nor sophisticated critiques of the Puritan Ethic, therefore, can destroy the elemental physiological and psychological truth that work within the marketplace is essential to being human under capitalism.

The case of the college professor is most revealing in this respect, for he has come to be accepted as a full member of the system in good standing in direct proportion as he has become an expert and an advisor concerned to rationalize and sustain the system. Or, in Loren Baritz's phrase, as he has become a servant of established power. But in becoming less alienated within the system, the professor has alienated himself from the classic conception of the scholar as a man whose essential commitment is to transcending known truth rather than to refining established revelation.

It is of course true that the conception of meaningful or productive work would be very much different under socialism than it is under capitalism. Work as the production of material goods for sustenance and convenience would occupy a marginal place in a socialist society. The reason for this is very simple: a truly socialist community would seize upon cybernated production as the way to free men and women from work in the traditional capitalist sense. The production of necessities, and of a dramatically extended range of conveniences, would be made as automatic as possible precisely in order to unchain men from such a narrow conception of meaningful activity.

Work would become transformed into any act which manifested the individual's or the group's urge and need to express its creative powers, and to extend and strengthen its relationships with nature and with other human beings. Men would still have to be educated for such work. Indeed, the process of evolving and implementing such an educational program would be one of the first and major tasks of any socialist leadership that came to power in an advanced country. But instead of providing various kinds of vocational training, such education would involve helping people become integrated personalities capable of freeing and using their capacities and powers in a creative manner.

Today, however, under American capitalism, creative work is primarily defined as a job in the marketplace system. Hence the dehumanization of that job, or the outright loss of such employment, plays a central causative role in alienation. Some of the most helpful insights into, and feeling for, the way such dehumanization takes place can be gained from reviewing what happens in a relatively small — even minor — episode in the general process of automating and cybernating the economy under existing conditions.

Consider, for example, the sequence of events which occurs as a bank shifts to a system which handles checks and accounts through machines which read the account numbers printed in contemporary hieroglyphics on each check.* The customer is immediately affected because his signature is no longer sufficient warranty on his check. He must buy special checks imprinted with the symbols that the machine can read. And, should he fail to use such a check, he must of course pay an extra fee for the special handling his individuality

*This story was related by the vice president of a bank, in the course of a long conversation about the displacement of people in modern industry.

requires. The irony, of course, is that these new checks are heralded as "Personalized Banking," whereas they actually represent a process which progressively de-personalizes the entire set of relationships. This is a small, but—precisely for that reason—particularly revealing example of how far the inversion of meaning has already proceeded within the existing system. The need to purchase such impersonalized checks is a minor result of the new procedures, but it does symbolize other consequences which are more serious.

In over-the-counter transactions, and in some other operations, tellers and other clerks still review the checks visually, *but the system is based on machines and numbers rather than upon people and signatures*. "The troubles begin," one banker explained, "when the clerks begin to act on this and start watching the style of the numbers instead of the signatures and the faces. People don't like being forgotten for numbers. We get lots of complaints. And there's a whole new kind of forgery and embezzlement based on this reliance on numbers." Such changes in the modern bank do not rival in drama or significance the effects of automation or cybernation on a larger scale. But for that very reason they do serve to underscore the dehumanization of the work itself and the alienation of the people involved.

The examples of the alienation inherent in serious underemployment and unemployment are almost unlimited. "I guess we've got the worries," one such man said of himself and his wife. "We've got the worries about running out of cash, about going to somebody and asking for something, about going on welfare. We've got the worries about the doctor bill. . .getting sick and the hospital and all that. And then," he added in a final, wrenching comment, "we've got the worries about time, about all that time to do the worrying."

Or consider the man who had to hang his half-loaf of dried bread on a string from the ceiling.

"Why?" he was asked.

"On account of the rats. I can't leave nuthin' on the table."

Such a man, and there are many, is so alienated that his principal relationships are with the problems of literal survival rather than with people—let alone creative work.

Other people in similar circumstances offer simple, blunt expressions of their knowledge that they are on the edge of human life.

"I'm about as far as I can go"—from an older coal miner out of work over two years.

"I want more than just to exist"—from a fourteen-year-old girl who has eaten nothing but surplus commodities for a year.

And still others, who have some employment, try to maintain a precarious hold on their identity by overlooking the way they are cheated by merchants. They are so caught in the definition of existence as the possession of things that they spend their meager funds on non-essentials in order to salvage what appears to be their self-esteem. Knowing this psychology of the fringe-man, the businessmen charge them more or give them shoddy goods. Others treated the same way have given up even the struggle for such false esteem. They know they are cheated, but their only comment is an apathetic shrug.

But perhaps the simplest and most telling expression of this alienation came in October 1963 from a man in Seattle.

"I have been out of work for nine months. I feel like half a man."

Half a man in Seattle and an astronaut on the board of directors of a bank in Texas. Those contrasts offer two of the most significant manifestations of alienation in mid-twentieth-century American capitalism. On the one hand, a man with no job who is conscious that he is but half a man. On the other hand, a man who has found the myriad challenges and rewards of being America's first spaceman so insufficient unto his wholeness that he seeks fulfillment by donning the flannel of the financier. In the first example, the failure of the system is dramatized overtly in a routine form. The second instance disguises an equal failure as a great achievement. There can be few more telling illustrations of alienation. The transformation of a vast social adventure into a mundane business operation reveals how far man's imagination and commitment have been crippled by marketplace values and practices.

Many mental disturbances are but manifestations of alienation. To be sure, mental illness is not peculiar to capitalism, but that does not exclude capitalism as a cause. It means that capitalism has not established an environment which supports human beings in their search for integration and wholeness. The poet William Carlos Williams once commented that "the pure products of America go crazy." He was suggesting that the sustained confrontation between, on the one hand, a commitment to the ideals and values of America and, on the other hand, the widespread evidence of the failure to honor and realize those axioms, would create a grave neurosis or a psychosis. His proposition was of course one-sided. He neglected the alternative of disengagement with the ideals and values.

In this connection, moreover, Marx's analysis of increasing misery is supported by the evidence that the poor are far less ready to respond to treatment for psychological illness. Their difficulties win them attention and care they have never before known, and they further resist help because the work and the society which awaits them on being cured offers little if any promise of a meaningful and purposeful sanity. "What sort of society is it, in truth," Marx asked, "where one finds several million in deepest loneliness. . .?" Certainly his answer, that it was not truly a society, let alone a community, has not received a ringing rebuttal in the record of psychological disturbance in the United States.

Nor in the evidence concerning the Negro. Or youth. Or women. Or even, for that matter, the fully employed white male. No white man can know the economic and psychological misery of being a Negro in the United States. He can learn about it. He can, depending upon his own sensitivity, feel varying degrees of empathy with and for it. And he can carry his share of the struggle to change that horror that passes for citizenship. But he can never know that alienation of the Negro. The white man can, however, become excruciatingly conscious of the alienation that he as the white man has suffered as a consequence of this treatment of the Negro. Whether or not he does become aware of it – and whatever his money income or his total wealth – he has in any event been alienated from the human condition to a considerable extent by this facet of American capitalism.

In a similar way, parents (and even childless adults) must endure the particular alienation that comes as part of realizing that large elements of contemporary youth reject major aspects of the society that the parents have created. Juvenile delinquency is but the most dramatic form of – and the most popular euphemism for – the increasing misery of youth in a society that has failed to sustain meaningful models of maturity and adulthood. In this connection, the beatniks and the gangs should not be misunderstood or over-emphasized.

The beats are perhaps the most alienated of all; human beings so nearly crushed as to be reduced more nearly to passive indifference than to passive resistance, and to confusing creativity with uninhibited exercise of the naked ego. Their personal experiences are unquestionably real and intense, and their small groups far more vital than many critics have allowed, but their sub-culture is not based on values that are capable of creatively transforming society. Picture the beats as the leaders of a newly independent but underdeveloped society and perhaps the point will be apparent.

For their part, the gangs are created by humans driven to organized violence in a kind of paradoxical corporate nihilism. They are not only rebels without a cause, they are rebels without even a coherent critique of the existing system. They fight over turf and women in the same spirit displayed by the ruthless entrepreneurs of a not-so-ancient American age. The most devastating commentary on their existence in the United States is that they have lived out the devolution so vividly portrayed in *Lord of the Flies* without ever having left home. It has not been necessary for them to be marooned on an island in order to demonstrate that a society based on Hobbesian beliefs will produce Hobbesian individuals. The moderating influences in such a society are ultimately transformed into Hobbesian influences through the inherent dynamism of the system. Thus a total, encompassing pressure molds the individual in that image.

Another sizable group of American youth has sought to define its alienation in terms of a succession of intense personal experiences. This is positive in the sense that it reveals a kind of intuitive reaction against the dehumanization and the lack of community in contemporary American society. Sexual promiscuity, for example, is less a permissive extension of learning by doing, or the result of a campus revival of the orgy, than the most dramatic sign of a sad and desperate search for a human relationship. There is cause for anguish in the inability to realize in advance that the means will in many, many cases blunt and scar the very sensitivity they seek, but the real tragedy lies in the responsibility of the adult world for treating sex as a commodity.

Indeed, the searing irony involved in the effort of these youths to rebel and find meaning through sex lies in their failure to see that they are really accepting the very definition of sex as sublimation that has been established and approved by the present order. The logic of the Freudian insight that sexual fulfillment is blocked by the existing system points to a drastic restructuring of the system so that Eros — love in *all* its manifestations — can replace and transcend (though not exclude) the merely sexual. But this has been subtly distorted and warped so that sexual activity separated from Eros has become one of the principal phenomena presented as proof that the established order provides fulfillment.

In this respect, at any rate, the youthful rebels are essentially conventional without even realizing it. For to equate resistance and rebellion with sex, and to define the sexual relationship as the essence of relationship per se, is ultimately to say that the identity of the companion is incidental save as measured on a rudimentary scale of crude physiological response. And it is to substitute changing partners in bed for changing society in such a way that a partnership in bed becomes a continuing culmination of a deepening and transforming relationship between two specific human beings in a community.

Marx had a very keen insight into this issue when he noted that revolutionaries might easily make the mistake, in their attacks upon capitalism, or in the early stages of a change from capitalism, of defining the sexual emancipation of men and women as wholesale promiscuity. As he realized, such an attitude involved little more than a projection of the capitalist fetishism of commodities; it was merely a definition of liberation in terms of sex as physical possession. The point is not the arbitrary desirability of pre-marital chastity, or of similar aspects of such a code; it is rather that which constitutes a truly human conception of a meaningful sexual relationship. And to define that as being independent of the nature of the non-sexual human relationship is to define sex as a branch of mechanics and thermodynamics.

Another segment of alienated youth seems to sense this crucial interrelation of all aspects of community, and is groping for a more positive and creative basis for an alternate culture and society. A significant number, for example, have joined the integration move-ment, and have helped provide the push that has carried a segment of that uprising to the threshold of a broader and more inclusive outlook and program. They recognize that making the Negro equal in the marketplace is only the first step in transforming the marketplace into a community of human beings. Along with others, they are beginning to revitalize American radicalism by denying the weary insistence of their erstwhile radical elders that it is impossible to change the world. They are insisting, not merely that it *can* be changed, but that it *must* be changed.

And still others, as with those in the so-called underworld of the hot-rod and the custom car, are struggling to create new varieties of art. The car builders are attempting to find a form appropriate to the changing role of the automobile in America. As they do so, moreover, they are giving lessons in engineering, and imaginative design, to the men from Detroit who arrive unannounced (and somewhat furtively) in their workshops. If the car survives as a means of mass transpor-tation, which is not at all probable, it will do so because these alienated youth of today will have won a participating role in the new society of tomorrow. It seems more likely that they will transform the auto into an occasionally mobile expression of an individual's experiments with form, space, and power. The hot-rods, after all, have already become the poor man's space vehicles.

It may be, however, that the state and condition of the con-temporary American woman offers the most striking example of alienation in advanced capitalism. For, in defining emancipation in precisely the terms that describe the condition of males in a capi-talist political economy, the female alienates herself from the pos-sibility of transforming the American family and society in a truly human and creative way. She forsakes the central human community for the impersonal marketplace without even entertaining the idea of transforming the marketplace into a co-operative community.

The alienation in such an act is matched only by the staggering lack of imagination displayed in the wholehearted acceptance by the female of the very image that she claims destroyed her identity and creativity. This would seem so far from being emancipation as to raise the question of whether or not women have not even alienated themselves from their vaunted intuition. For the essence of what they define as emancipation is the right to function as males in the marketplace. Yet the men are the reason the women advance as the explanation of their need for emancipation. A meaningful conception of emancipation, on the other hand, would evolve from the idea and ideal of creative partnership between males and females in a co-operative community organized on principles of equity transcending the axioms of possessive individualism competing in the marketplace.

IV. AT HOME: PROLETARIANIZATION –
THE CRUSHING OF SENSITIVITY AND UTOPIA,
AND THE DENIAL OF PARTICIPATION

> *W*andering between two worlds, one
> dead,
> The other powerless to be born.
>
> Matthew Arnold,
> *Stanzas from the Grand Chartreuse*

IN A very real sense, the woman in acting on her existing definition of emancipation is facilitating what Marx would have called her own proletarianization. For contrary to what most people assume or believe, Marx meant a good deal more by proletarianization than simply working for wages on the assembly line in an urban manufacturing plant. In the structural sense, and hence in his view primarily, he meant the loss of any participating role in the principal decisions of the capitalist marketplace due to the loss of control over any private property which played a part in the productive activities of the system. The overt sign of this loss of full citizenship was of course the change from entrepreneurial standing to the condition of wage labor.

In a political economy based upon the control of private property, with its law codified within that framework, the loss of productive private property also involves a fall into second-class citizenship. Marx understood that capitalism, like all social systems, includes a great deal more than economics. It is a complex network of procedures, habits, customs, rules, laws, institutions, and ideas. These elements modify — by reinforcing or limiting — the direct and immediate impact and effect of the specifically economic factors. But since the system is based upon, and operates through, the economic marketplace, an individual's position in the marketplace is crucial. It establishes basic limits upon his activity in other areas of the system, and it defines the opportunities open to him. Marx viewed proletarianization as the process, similar and related to alienation, whereby the individual was progressively excluded from full and effective participation in the political and social parts of the system as a result of his reduction to the position of wage laborer in the economic sphere. He was increasingly acted upon rather than participating in.

The only productive property available to the proletarian is his personal labor, and his wage is the price he receives for selling it in the market. He can organize in unions or increase his skills to better that price, but neither act transforms his property as labor into entrepreneurial property in the crucial meaning (or practice) of enterprise capitalism. He does not thereby gain directional control or authority over the use, or the basic return from the use, of private property owned by true capitalists. A cut of the profits, after all, is not a share in the central decisions of the enterprise. It is a passive role in an active venture.

It is true that Marx usually talked about the proletariat in terms of wage laborers on a factory assembly line, or workers who were even less happily placed in the system. He used those examples because they were the most common forms of wage labor during the time he produced the bulk of his analysis. But he never defined the proletariat per se in those restricted terms. He specifically included agricultural labor, service, and associated work, and in his last analyses explicitly pointed out that the rise of the corporation transformed an increasing proportion of supervisory and even administrative duties into wage labor. As he remarked in one memorable phrase, the supervisors also "walk the streets." The contemporary loss of influence (and job security) by middle management in large corporations is a further extension of the same process.

This is a crucial point because most people mistakenly think of proletarianization only in terms of being pushed or otherwise forced down into the dirtiest, hardest, and lowest-paid kind of industrial day-labor. They conclude, therefore, that proletarianization has drastically decreased, and that Marx was wrong. But these particular features of the principal example of proletarianization used by Marx to dramatize the issue in his own time do not define proletarianization per se. Proletarianization concerns the general condition of the wage laborer in terms of his humanity and his sensitivity, and in terms of his lack of participation in the formulation of alternatives and in choosing between them.

Hence the line of proletarianization is not defined by any particular functional or income boundaries in the system. It may roughly coincide with different functional or income lines at various times in the course of industrialization, but it is basically independent of such categories. In the United States, as in other advanced industrial societies, the moving line of proletarianization has in recent years been climbing up the functional and income ladder. This means that many people who wear white collars (and Brooks Brothers suits) and blouses (or silk sheaths), and who are paid with monthly checks instead of in weekly pay envelopes, have become members of the structural proletariat.

This reality has been obscured by two concurrent phenomena. Gross dollar income (and, to a lesser degree, absolute income) have also been rising, and this improvement in the traditional capitalist criteria has been given more attention by the individual himself and by those who are concerned to maintain the fiction of an entrepreneurial system. Money and power *seem* to go together in a far more direct and causal relationship than they actually do under advanced capitalism, and the defenders of the established order invest considerable talent and energy in sustaining the vitality of this equation in the mind of the public. Since in truth there is some connection between the two categories, the campaign enjoys significant success. In addition, a similar effort has been made to characterize those functions which lack power with certain symbols and rituals which provide the semblance of power. Indeed, many people who are aware of their lack of leverage co-operate in the illusion as a way of coming to terms with the reality of their inferior position. The status-seekers are more often people who know (or sense) that they do not have power, rather than people who have lost it — or are in the process of losing it. The latter are far more concerned with the realities than with the symbols.

Neither of these factors changes the reality that the line of proletarianization is moving up the functional and income scales. There are many examples of this, but the following illustrations seem particularly indicative of the process. The first concerns the poverty of power in the decision-making process of the system that is suffered by a significant number of people who make as much — and sometimes more — money as the people who possess the power. Major figures in the entertainment arena offer rather obvious examples of this situation. Even when they are connected with the shadow industry of big-time crime, their money is not the handmaiden of power. Marx called the living-dead of industrial slums the *lumpen* proletariat, and these entertainers might in the same vein be called the macaroni proletariat.

A second illustration is offered by those functional groups which once enjoyed power and influence, but which have steadily lost them in the process of advancing industrialization. The self-contained family farmer comes readily to mind in this instance, but he has many parallels in the urban sector of the economy. The small banker, grocery store owner, and clothier provide similar case histories. And, since the end of World War II, these men have been joined in their slow but persistent decline in influence by many manufacturers and entrepreneurs in the service industries. Each of these men may make more money, but they have been pushed to the fringes of the decision-making community, and they play a far less influential role in politics as well as in economics.

Still another example is social in nature and concerns the increasing rate of juvenile delinquency among middle- and upper-income families, whose male heads also inhabit functional groups which are relatively high in the system. It may be, indeed, that this upward movement of the delinquency line is one of the most accurate indicators of the similar change in the line of proletarianization. For, in this connection, the shift points to two very significant phenomena: a breakdown in the role of the parents (and particularly the father) as a meaningful, relevant, and consequential model for influencing the environment; and a turn by the youth away from any such model into defiance of – and an assault upon – the system per se. Viewed as a *social* phenomenon, delinquency thus appears as an early, crude, and unconceptualized consciousness of the increasing proletarianization of American society.* The youth are in some respects rebelling against the acquiescence of the adults, as well as against their general loss of leverage within the structure of the system.

A final example is directly related to such delinquency and involves the use of free time by the adult population. The connection with delinquency arises because one of the failures of the adults is to provide any meaningful direction for the creative use of that free time and thus transpose it into true leisure. One delinquent made the point this way:

"Sure, man. Lotsa what we do is a drag. We know it better'n you. Why ya think we end up rumblin' so much. But, man! – What you squares do! That's an even bigger drag. Mosta ya sit 'round watchin' things. Or bitchin' at things without doin' nothin'. We're at least movin'."

The cut goes to the bone. The free time available to the adult ceases to be free, because he uses most of it in an almost compulsive activity involving only minor and incidental enlargement of his mind, emotions, or relationships. Most of it can accurately be described as the ruthless pursuit of petty ecstacies. It is unfair, however, to assign all the blame to the individual. True enough, some manage to break out of the pattern, but only the very strongest can win that freedom. The reason for this, as Herbert Marcuse has recently pointed out in his perceptive essay on *One-Dimensional Man,* lies in the power

*This is not at all to discount the individual psychological and physiological factors involved in delinquency. But those elements operate, and must therefore be understood, within a particular structural framework.

of the system to define the choices and impose them upon the individual. The alternatives are often pleasant enough in their own right, and might in some cases even become creatively rewarding if chosen by the individual on his own terms and for his own reasons.

But the capitalist dynamic has turned free time into another marketplace for the consumer-goods industry, in which all the products have the effect of keeping the individual busy using things rather than occupied extending himself. The result is to extend the alienation of man from himself, and from other men, that is inherent in the marketplace. Modes of behavior are substituted for creative activity, and free time becomes so far removed from the classical conception of leisure as to be unrecognizable. The resulting total organization of the individual's life is non-terroristic, but it is nonetheless totalitarian. Indeed, the contemporary American use of free time might appropriately be characterized as a very complicated adaptation for adults of the child's game of follow-the-leader.

It is quite true, of course, that most Americans are not fully conscious of this increasing proletarianization of their system. But this is not at all to the principal point that Marx was making in his analysis of capitalism. He was saying first of all that the process of proletarianization steadily includes more individuals. He very carefully explained that class consciousness was an evolutionary — not an instantaneous — phenomenon. And he grew ever more aware of, and impressed by, the negative power of the original capitalist utopia to block recognition of the new reality created by capitalism itself. The original vision became a delusion; but in some ways it thereby extended its sway over men's minds. This was particularly the case as the information marketplace became increasingly controlled by a few entrepreneurs. They effectively merchandized the delusion by defining capitalism as an abundance of consumer goods. This was a classic distortion whereby the issue of participation in the primary decisions of the system was transformed into the question of which gadget to buy.

There are some significant indications, however, that there is an increasing consciousness of the underlying structural proletarianization of American society. Perhaps the most striking example involves the rise of what is so mistakenly called the radical right. This active and articulate portion of the population includes the Birchites, the less extreme but no less agitated followers of Senator Barry Goldwater, and the leaders and members of other similar groups.

These people are conscious that the effective economic, political, and social power of individual private property has been declining at an increasing rate since the 1890's, and more particularly since World War I. Marx anticipated that such an awareness would arise among individual entrepreneurs (and others who shared their outlook, whatever their momentary position as property holders) as the corporation came to dominate the capitalist marketplace, and as the corporation turned ever more to the government for assistance in sustaining the system.

But, with his typical preference for the jugular phrase, Marx called them reactionary. He was correct. They are reactionary because they want to turn the system back to the time of their real and imagined leadership. They are not radical because they do not strike to the heart of the problem. The root issue is not how to restore entrepreneurial capitalism, but rather how to transcend the achievements and failures of corporation capitalism and create a moral, equitable, and co-operative community. There can be no doubt, on the other hand, that these reactionaries are intensely and perceptively conscious of the structural changes within capitalism that Marx saw as producing increasing proletarianization. They are class conscious to a high degree. And they are not, as so often is asserted, merely seeking status. They want to recover, maintain, and use the power they once enjoyed and exercised.

Another segment of the population which is becoming increasingly conscious of the basic proletarianization of the system is made up of those Negroes and whites who have come to understand that equality in the marketplace will not solve the problems of either the Negro (and other colored peoples) or the whites. These men and women have become steadily more class conscious in this fundamental respect. Part of this awareness has no doubt evolved out of the steady application of Christian insights and judgments by such Negro leaders as the Reverend Martin Luther King, Jr., but more of it has come from hard, painful experience in the reality of the system itself. While these people have not developed any integrated or detailed alternatives to the existing system, it is clear that they are consciously moving in that direction. No less than the farmers of Kansas between 1900 and 1914, these Americans could also become socialists.

Just this possibility is one of the factors that has served to increase the class consciousness of still another group within American society. Coupled with their intimate knowledge of the advancing structural proletarianization of the system, the radicalism inherent in the entire Negro issue has prompted a sizable element of the upper-class decision-making community to confront the problem more directly and openly than they did even during the Great Depression. Few of these leaders are openly admitting that Marx was correct. But neither Freud nor Marx would have expected them to do so. They are nevertheless discussing the problem within the broad framework that Marx established.

They are concerned, that is to say, with the structural weaknesses of the economic system and with the social and political tensions that have accompanied the evolution of those soft spots. Not too surprisingly, they recommend that the giant corporation accept an increasing share of responsibility for the social and the political, as well as the economic, functioning of the system. A good many of them openly compare the present age with the era of mercantilism, and go on to call for a similar integration of the private and governmental decision-making communities. The proposals of the rest fall into the same pattern. The system, they argue must be administered as a tightly co-ordinated and administered unit.

As this approach implies, most of these men are elitists. Candidly or otherwise, they advocate further restricting the areas in which the citizenry exercises significant influence in and upon the decision-making process. As with other reactions to the increasing structural proletarianization of the system, this attitude of the upper-class leadership raises the fundamental question of whether or not American capitalism has created — or can create — an ethical and equitable community. That question lies at the very center of Marx's critique.

FOUR

*C*apitalism and the Creation
of an Ethical and Equitable Community

I. CAPITALISM AS POSSESSIVE,
COMPETITIVE INDIVIDUALISM

> *Honourable* is whatsoever possession, action, or quality, is an argument and signe of Power. . . .Riches are Honourable; for they are Power. . . .Covetousnesse of great Riches, and ambition of great Honours, are Honourable; as signes of power to obtain them. . . .Nor does it alter the case of Honour, whether an action (so it be great and difficult, and consequently a signe of much power,) be just or unjust: for Honour consisteth onely in the opinion of Power.
>
> Thomas Hobbes,
> *Leviathan,* Chapter 10

> *T*he great and *chief end* therefore, of Men uniting into Commonwealths, and putting themselves under Government, *is the Preservation of their Property.*
>
> John Locke,
> *Two Treatises of Government;*
> *Second Treatise,* Section 124

*A*s indicated by his central concern with alienation and proletarianization, Marx's critique of capitalism hinged upon its failure to create and sustain an ethical and equitable community. All capitalism did, in his view, was create a system of political economy and a society. His career as an economist was the result of his intellectual commitment to find out whether or not this inability was inherent in the nature of capitalism, and he concluded that it was indigenous. Hence the culmination of any discussion of Marx in connection with America (or vice versa) is a confrontation on this fundamental issue.

The first requirement in making an evaluation is a clear understanding of the standard of judgment employed by Marx. As a few commentators like George Lichtheim have noted, Marx's ideal of man, citizenship, and community derived from the classic Greek example and from the best in the later Western image of the aristocrat. The foundation of this conception of Man is what contemporary psychologists like Herbert Maslow and S. I. Hayakawa call the integrated personality. It is a man fully aware of himself, his obligations and duties, and his creative capacities, but equally conscious of the extent to which this recognition of oneself and powers is a product of social (and moral) relationships with other human beings in a community.

"Human emancipation will be complete," Marx explained, "only when the actual existing individual man takes back into himself the abstract citizen." "Only in community with others," he continued, "has each individual the means of cultivating his gifts in all directions; only in community, therefore, is personal freedom possible." "The question," he pointed out in a profound insight, "is whether special interest shall represent political intelligence or whether political intelligence shall represent special interest." In the good state, he concluded, "political intelligence will regulate the ownership of land according to the maxims of the State, it will not regulate the maxims of the State according to the ownership of land; it will enforce the ownership of land not according to its private egoism, but according to its civic nature."

Capitalism destroyed the ideal, as well as the reality, of that kind of citizenship and community. "Man's self-esteem, freedom," Marx therefore insisted, "must be awakened once more. Only this feeling, which disappeared from the world with the Greeks, and from the blue mists of heaven with Christianity, can once more make from society a fellowship of men working for their highest purposes, a democratic State." The issue was not how much men owned, but rather what they made, the conditions of its production, the principles of its distribution, the nature of the relationships men had with each other in the course of those activities, and what they did after their material wants had been met. From these standards and these objectives, and not from an economist's demand curves, Marx derived his basic credo: "I call revolution the conversion of all hearts and the raising of all hands on behalf of the honor of the free man, the free State which belongs to no master, but which is itself a public being."

Marx argued that the inability of capitalism to create such individuals and such a community was inherent in the psychological and general theory of possessive individualism which underlay the entire system. This conception of the world, or *Weltanschauung*, was a massive mural painted by three men during the years when Christianity and feudalism lost their persuasiveness and effectiveness, as the known world grew faster than those conceptions of reality could cope with the new reality. These giant mapmakers of Western capitalism were Thomas Hobbes, John Locke, and Adam Smith. Hobbes explored and charted the main outline and features of this cosmos. Locke added new data and refinements. Smith codified the resulting system and cast his laws in economic terminology. Their combined labors created a definition and description of capitalist man and his society that can be summarized in the following principles.*

First. A man is human to the extent that he is free of dependence on the will of other men.

Second. This being the case, the individual's freedom can justifiably be limited only by those rules designed to secure the same freedom for others.

Third. Freedom from this constraint means the liberty to avoid all relations save those the individual enters into on a voluntary basis with a view to his own interest.

Fourth. Individuals basically own their persons and capabilities; they have no essential or prior obligation or debt to society.

Fifth. The individual cannot consign or convey his whole person, but he can assign his ability and talents to work.

Sixth. Interpersonal relations are therefore contracts involving the consignment of this ability to work; or, in other words, market relations, and society is the sum of such market relations.

Seventh. Politics is the process of maintaining the conditions for orderly exchange between individuals defined as owning themselves.

Eighth. Once such a framework has been established, there is little need for compulsion. Regularized market exchanges strengthen, deepen, and sustain the order without such coercion. Force is necessary only in dealing with what Locke called Unnatural Man; that is,

---

*My original formulation has benefited from revisions prompted by C. B. Macpherson, *The Political Theory of Possessive Individualism: Hobbes to Locke* (Oxford: Clarendon Press, 1962); S. S. Wolin, *Politics and Vision: Continuity and Innovation in Western Political Thought* (Boston: Little, Brown, 1960); and from conversations with Harvey Goldberg.

men who violate the principles of the system. These can be individuals who transgress the second axiom and attempt to subject the entire marketplace to their ego and will, or individuals who deny the validity of the first or fourth axioms and thereby challenge the premises of the entire system.*

The whole issue of capitalism's creation of an equitable and ethical community revolves around the consequences of this system of possessive individualism. On the one hand, the assumptions and the logic of their interrelationships provide great consistency and strength. Grant the central principles and the system hangs together and generates vast changes. On the other hand, there is no way to escape or fundamentally modify the market society once it has been agreed that man is a human being only as owner of himself, free in possession of himself. For this defines moral values as market values and transforms equity into the results produced through higgling at the bargain counter.

Marx clearly understood both the axioms and their logic. His counterattack was aimed at the jugular vein of the capitalist system. He pointed out that separating the empirical, egoistic, materialistic self from the social self resulted in defining human relations as competitive interaction. Men competed with each other for their freedom

*Adam Smith spoke on this point as follows: "According to the system of natural liberty, the sovereign has only three duties to attend to. . . .First, the duty of protecting the society from the violence and invasion of other independent societies; secondly, the duty of protecting, as far as possible, every member of the society from the injustice or oppression of every other member of it, or the duty of establishing an exact administration of justice; and, thirdly, the duty of erecting and maintaining certain public works and certain public institutions, which it can never be for the interest of any individual, or small number of individuals, to erect and maintain; because the profit could never repay the expense to any individual or small number of individuals, though it may frequently do much more than repay it to a great society." *Wealth of Nations,* Book IV, Chapter IX.

and for their very humanity. Yet the true nature of man made it impossible for individual men ever to achieve either freedom or humanity or community through a process of competition in the marketplace. They could attain those objectives only through affirming and cultivating their social and public life. The fatal flaw in capitalism, therefore, was its artificial definition of universal interests in terms of private, special interests.

"The freedom to exercise a craft," Marx pointed out, "is just the freedom to exercise a craft and no more." If this partial freedom is taken to be all of freedom, Marx added, then "the individual locks himself into his empirical nature against his eternal nature." Once this was done, there was no way for him to join other individuals in creating a truly ethical and equitable community. Capitalist man had thus defined himself outside such a possibility by declaring that his freedom was gained through competitive relations in the marketplace. Even if the marketplace expanded sufficiently to provide enough for all special interests, therefore, the individual would still remain a partially fulfilled man and there would be no community.

II. EFFORTS TO TRANSCEND THE SYSTEM:
"FEUDAL SOCIALISM"

*T*hou didst bring me forth for
all the Greeks in common, not
for thyself alone.

Euripides,
Iphigenia in Aulis

MARX was aware that a segment of capitalist society sensed or actually saw this failure of the system during the various stages or phases of its development. He also recognized that a minority of this minority tried to square the circle by creating a community out of the marketplace. While admitting that their efforts might ameliorate the harsh reality of the system, he denied that they could perform such alchemy. Showing a talent for the trenchant phrase that he indulged far too seldom, Marx formulated a nomenclature for these men and their ideas that was based on the kind of pairing of opposites that most Americans associate with the astringent social criticism of Thorstein Veblen.

Marx discussed the first such capitalist critics of capitalism under the heading of "Feudal Socialism." And of all such constellations of men and ideas, Marx probably had the most respect for this group and its argument. He was seriously troubled by their performance because he knew that feudalism was not, as so many Americans think it was, an unmitigated horror. He clearly understood the coercive side of feudalism, for example, and its low level of material well-being; but he did not judge those characteristics from the assumption or belief that they were unique to feudalism and had thereafter disappeared from the world — or that they were caused by evil men who cruelly confined modern technology to a dungeon in their castles.

"Neither capital nor labor appear untrammeled" under feudalism, he pointed out, but singly and in relation to the other were "defined by the corporate rules, by the conditions connected with them, and by the conceptions of professional duties, mastership, etc." He further acknowledged, as suggested by his remark about the blue mists of heaven associated with Christianity, that religion and the Church played a significant role in controlling capital and its use of property. As a result, and most important of all so far as Marx was concerned, feudalism did not divide men into a personal and a social self. Coerced and poor as he was, feudal man was still integrated. Marx saluted that achievement in a moving summary: "Folk life and civic life were identical."

Capitalism first cracked and finally sundered this integrated man. Marx insisted that this was fundamentally and ultimately destructive of man per se, even though it temporarily freed and fed his ego for the battle to conquer nature and thereby triumph in the struggle to rise about subsistence existence. But he also insisted that any effort to sustain or re-introduce feudal unity after capitalism had emerged was doomed to failure. The evidence suggests that Marx resisted this conclusion, and that he retained a kind of sympathy and admiration for his feudal socialists even as he damned them as irrelevant. It also seems clear that his study of such men struck one intellectual spark that deserves to be fanned into full flame.

This was his insight into the existence of a national class. Marx meant by this a segment of the ruling class which, under certain conditions and for a relatively short time, exercised its power and authority in a manner that actually did represent and advance the interests of the entire society. Marx unfortunately never developed and used this descriptive and analytical tool to any significant extent in his own work. Neither have his formal followers, nor others who ignore or belittle him publicly while ransacking his mind in the secrecy of their libraries. But with reference to American history, for example, this insight offers a fruitful approach to such men and movements as Jacksonian Democracy, Lincolnesque Republicanism, the Progressivism of Marcus Hanna, Theodore Roosevelt, Herbert Croly, and Woodrow Wilson, the outlook of Herbert Hoover, the New Deal of Franklin Delano Roosevelt, and the current efforts by the leaders of corporation capitalism to revitalize and sustain the system.

In the specific form of what Marx called feudal socialism, this national class appeared in the United States as what is generally known as the group called the Founding Fathers. To speak more precisely, the movement was composed of those men, actually spanning two generations, who adapted the axioms, attitudes, and policies of British Mercantilism to the American situation. Some of the key figures were Jonathan Edwards, George Washington, John Adams, James Madison, and John Quincy Adams. Those men, and others associated with them, were concerned to control the principles of possessive and competitive individualism by using the counterbalancing idea and ideal of the whole man obligated to other men within the framework of a true community that characterized the Christian feudal society. Their rhetoric, their policies, and their actions converged in an effort to build an equitable and ethical community within the limits of capitalist economics.

Though he never discussed this phase of American history, Marx did comment on British mercantilists within the framework of feudal socialism. Compared with what he characterized as the "helter-skelter" life of mid-nineteenth-century bourgeois society, Marx admitted that mercantilism "appears as a higher form" of capitalism. He pointed out its intimate relationship with Christianity, acknowledged its avowed commitment to the ideal of the whole man based on an aristocratic model, and recognized its political, social, and intellectual achievements as well as its success in organizing and carrying through the crucial first steps in developing a capitalist political economy at the national level. He also saluted the mercantilist critique of unrestrained capitalism. It was "bitter, witty and incisive criticism, striking the bourgeoisie to its very heart's core."

The slashing attacks by Edwards and the Adamses on the excesses of the unrestrained ego and the morality of the competitive marketplace certainly bear out Marx's insight into such mercantilism in the American context. His judgment is likewise verified by the emphasis those men placed on community. Edwards was a giant among those who cried out in pain and anger against the abandonment of the basic Christian injunction to "love thy neighbor as thyself." Suffering, he pointed out, results from man's failure to create a harmonious community, and is God's way of inciting action toward that goal. The real sin is to deny this, he insisted, and instead explain suffering as the result of sloth or laziness. The sin is to redefine the existing situation as the good state of man, and then proceed to exploit it for individual gain against one's neighbor.

John Quincy Adams likewise committed himself to a conception of the common good that had its roots in the Christian ideal of community. In the final analysis, moreover, he accepted the clear implication that Christian principles left the way open for men to organize their economic life in a manner that was different from the capitalist marketplace. "As the earth was given by the Creator to mankind in common," he pointed out, "the distribution of property in it is left to be settled among the human race, by physical force or by agreement, compact, covenant." Adams read Christian doctrine to mean that the general welfare took priority over individual gain. His program of planned and co-ordinated internal improvements, including educational and scientific development, was based on this central axiom. And, also, his opposition to slavery.

Washington's outlook was very similar. For that matter, Adams repeatedly identified himself as a disciple of the first President. Washington's grand vision of developing the country along a communications system running westward from the Potomac to the Mississippi was conceived in the thought and hope that it would free the Negro and unite the country as well as make it wealthy. And he openly and boldly warned his countrymen that they must commit themselves to an ideal of community to have any chance of avoiding disaster.

Other early leaders, such as Madison and Albert Gallatin, may have been less intensely and formally religious, but they shared the same fundamental view of the world. Gallatin's magnificent Report on Roads and Canals, presented to the Senate on April 6, 1808, after two years of extensive preparation, was perhaps the crowning manifestation of this *Weltanschauung*. Explicitly designed to create the physical and economic basis for a "more intimate community of interests" among the people of the nation through the national planning and construction of a vast network of communications, the proposal amounted to an American Ten-Year Plan that gives a particularly appropriate tone to Marx's nomenclature of "Feudal Socialism." Along with the plans advanced by Washington and Adams, it also serves to clarify the crucial difference between the conception of internal improvements held by those men and the local and uncoordinated plans advocated by the leaders of bourgeois capitalism under the banner of Jacksonian Democracy.

On the other hand, Marx was wrong in discounting so completely the significance and influence of the mercantilists as their power began to wane. His charge that they displayed a "total incapacity to comprehend the march of modern history," and his view that their efforts therefore amounted to no more than a "literary battle," are mistaken. They understood very well indeed precisely what was happening, that the view of the world as a competitive marketplace was displacing their own more integrated and balanced outlook, and they offered incisive analyses of that change and astute warnings about the consequences.

John Quincy Adams, to name but one outstanding example, displayed a shrewd intelligence and a great courage in the course of refusing to abandon the battlefield of politics and ideology to the new *Weltanschauung*. He and others were aware that they were losing ground to the spirit and the power of unrestrained bourgeois capitalism, and understood that they would very probably fail to block that turn in what Marx called "the march of modern history." But they also realized, or sensed, that capitalism would sooner or later have to return to a confrontation with the issues they raised, and in that essential respect they understood the march of history quite as well as Marx himself.

It is even more impressive to realize that a few of them, like Madison and John Quincy Adams, came to appreciate the specific and central weaknesses in their outlook that Marx spotted and emphasized in his critique. One of these, of course, was the existence of slavery. No true community could be established, by mercantilism any more than by bourgeois capitalism or any other social system, until that institution was destroyed and the Negro admitted into full citizenship. Men like Madison and Adams knew that mercantilism would fail unless it resolved that basic contradiction between their ideals and the American reality.

They won the opening rounds, moreover, when slavery was excluded from the Northwest Territory, and when the slave trade was terminated. And they came very near attaining a crucial victory during the slavery debates of 1828 – 1832 in Virginia. It is one of the great ironies of American history that John Quincy Adams's courageous and influential efforts to end slavery were conceived and undertaken with the intention and hope of producing a drastically different society than the one which ultimately emerged from the war between the North and the South. His ideal and goal of a community which included the Negro was certainly lost – if not actually denied – in the individualistic capitalism that emerged triumphant from the Civil War.

The degree to which the mercantilists implicitly and explicitly defined the egoistic part of man in terms of possessive individualism and competitive marketplace economics created another soft spot in their system. This is by no means the only way in which that half of man can be defined; but once that delineation is accepted, then the ego seems almost certain to subvert the social part of man that the mercantilists sought to protect and preserve, and to glorify in action. For if the ego is defined in that way, the ego cannot accept serious, continuing restrictions upon itself in the competitive marketplace without denying itself in the very arena in which it is supposed to find fulfillment.

American mercantilists failed to grapple with this contradiction in their philosophy either as directly or as effectively as they tried to cope with the issue of slavery. In this sense, of course, they contributed to the great difficulties they encountered in holding off the triumph of their opponents who stressed the narrower conception of man and freedom as defined by the marketplace. Ultimately, of course, they were unable to prevent that change. Marx accurately noted their failure, but he underestimated their prior achievements and discounted too heavily the tradition that the mercantilists had created. They left an idea and an approach which influenced Europeans and Americans in the twentieth century.

Marx was correct, however, in pointing out that an expansionist foreign policy played a crucial role in the efforts of the mercantilists to maintain their more balanced system and to sustain their ideal of community. Madison and others argued that such expansion would control the tension between the individualistic and the social halves of man by providing enough resources and opportunities to satisfy the demands of the ego, and enough space to absorb the demagogic energies of any would-be dictators. What expansion actually did, of course, was to strengthen the definition of community as a competitive marketplace, and that further weakened the social half of man save as it defined that part of man in terms of militant, emotional nationalism. And that spirit destroys community – and communities – in the name of obedience. As he came to understand such consequences of expansion, John Quincy Adams gradually turned against it as the means of sustaining the American community. A small minority supported him, but they were unable to establish and win general acceptance for such a modified mercantilism.

The result was the full victory of competitive capitalism with the election of Andrew Jackson, and the vigorous expansion of the marketplace through the annexation of Oregon, the War against Mexico, and ultimately the Civil War itself. This acquisition, exploitation, and development of a continental marketplace created a burgeoning capitalism that outproduced any other unit in the world capitalist system within the short time span of two generations. Marx was undeniably accurate in emphasizing the power, and what he called "the civilizing sides," of this bourgeois capitalism. Whatever its costs, it finally created a mighty and productive economy and transformed an unsettled continent into a national society.

III. EFFORTS TO TRANSCEND THE SYSTEM:
"BOURGEOIS SOCIALISM"

---

*C*laim your right, your unquestioned right, to equal participation.

> John W. Vethake,
> *The Doctrine of*
> *Anti-Monopoly,* 1835

▼

*T*he people's party. . .demands equal opportunities and exact justice in business for each individual and proposes to abolish all monopolistic privileges and power.

> *Farmer's Alliance,*
> Lincoln, Nebraska,
> October 22, 1891

LIKE mercantilism before it, the successes of bourgeois capitalism carried it to a point where it had either to modify itself fundamentally in order to create a community, or enter upon a further expansion of the marketplace in the hope of sustaining some balance between the egoistic and the social halves of men in the United States. Prior to that terminal crisis, between the late 1820's and the 1890's, the reformers who attempted to meet and resolve this tension were the men and women whom Marx called "Bourgeois Socialists." He classified them in two broad categories—agrarian and urban—in keeping with the shift from a predominantly agricultural to an industrial society. The differences in their outlooks and programs were significant, but they shared the underlying objectives of establishing some controls over possessive individualism and some checks on the ruthless operation of the competitive marketplace, and of opening—and keeping open—the marketplace itself.

Marx freely acknowledged the positive results achieved by this coalition of what he called "liberal economists, philanthropists, humanitarians, improvers of the condition of the working class," and others, such as the abolitionists, who were concerned with "redressing social grievances." They laid bare "the disastrous effects" of "the concentration of capital and land in a few hands," "of overproduction and crises," and "pointed out the inevitable ruin of the petty bourgeois and [small farmers], the misery of the proletariat, the anarchy in production, the crying inequalities in the distribution of wealth, the industrial war of extermination between nations, [and] the dissolution of old moral bonds, of the old family relations, [and] of the old nationalities."

These men and women significantly mitigated many of the harsh, inhuman, and dehumanizing aspects of bourgeois capitalism. They sought a more equal distribution of property and opportunity through such measures as anti-monopoly laws, homestead legislation, the relaxation of punishment for debt and bankruptcy, and various pieces of monetary legislation designed to help and sustain the smaller entrepreneur. As symbolized in their respective styles by Andrew Jackson and William Jennings Bryan, these men were trying to broaden—and keep broadened—the definition and the number of businessmen within American capitalism.

Bryan captured the essence of bourgeois socialism in one classic paragraph he used to establish the central theme of his famous Cross of Gold Speech. "We say to you that you have made the definition of a business man too limited in its application. The man who is employed for wages is as much a business man as his employer; the attorney in a country town is as much a business man as the corporation counsel in a great metropolis; the merchant at the cross-roads store is as much a business man as the merchant of New York; the farmer who goes forth in the morning and toils all day, who begins in the spring and toils all summer, and who by the application of brain and muscle to the natural resources of the country creates wealth, is as much a business man as the man who goes upon the Board of Trade and bets upon the price of grain; the miners who go down a thousand feet into the earth, or climb two thousand feet upon the cliffs, and bring forth from their hiding places the precious metals to be poured into the channels of trade are as much business men as the few financial magnates who, in a back room, corner the money of the world. We come to speak of this broader class of business men. . . . What we need is an Andrew Jackson to stand, as Jackson stood, against the encroachments of organized wealth."

Such reformers also supplied ideas and important support for the national class that developed during this phase of American capitalism. In the early years, as it arose in the small and medium-sized entrepreneurial operators of the North and West, this national class based its ideology on a modified version of the physiocratic doctrine as stated by Thomas Jefferson and John Taylor of Caroline. The wealth and social standing of such of its leaders as Jackson and Martin Van Buren were accurately interpreted at the time as symbols of the achievements that were possible within the system. As the cotton and slave culture expanded westward, however, it divided the West into slavery and non-slavery elements. The bourgeois national class fractured along that line. The pure and committed bourgeoisie judged slavery a serious challenge to the competitive position of the free entrepreneur, and to the central definition of free-dom as the liberty and power to alienate his labor in keeping with his own definition of his own interest.

These men ultimately reorganized the national class of bourgeois capitalism around the Republican party under the leadership of William E. Seward and Abraham Lincoln. Its central objectives were to extend the definition of freedom as possessive individualism in the marketplace economy to the entire system, to facilitate the develop-ment of the marketplace as an economic system per se, and to open the way for various elements of society to enter the marketplace as participating members – or to retain their existing membership. These objectives required either the acquiescence of the South or its defeat in war. Lincoln stated and offered this choice, explicitly refusing to extend the traditional compromise in which slavery and non-slavery elements shared the development of the marketplace.

Southerners feared the results of limiting slavery to its existing boundaries just as much as the Northern bourgeois entrepreneurs feared its extension westward across the Mississippi. They were thus inclined to view the proposal offered by Lincoln as a diabolic refine-ment on Hobson's Choice in which the horse next in line was not only less than perfect, but was actually incapable of carrying a man at all. The resulting and successful war to coerce the South, during which the bourgeois definition of freedom was formally extended to the entire society through the Emancipation Proclamation, raised the central issue of whether or not the new freedmen should be given property as part of being admitted to the marketplace society.

A minority of leaders within the triumphant national class ad-vocated this course. They held that the Negro had earned such prop-erty through his labor as a slave, labor which had under the principles of possessive individualism created a moral claim on the property. In addition, of course, their emotions of vengeance and their political ambitions served to reinforce this moral and policy argument. A majority of the leadership successfully opposed this approach. They held that the act of freeing the Negro gave him full citizenship because it gave him control of his person; and that he could thereafter participate as a free man in the system on an equal basis with all other men.

This was a stronger and more cogent argument than later commentators have often allowed. For the definition of humanity and freedom which is both inherent and explicit in possessive individualism offers no basis for creating special exceptions on the grounds of historical experience. The necessity and the obligation to extend and establish the principles are clear beyond doubt. Those had been met, furthermore, by freeing the Negro and admitting him to the marketplace. But if the process of compensating special groups for past failures is once begun, or the practice of establishing newcomers in the marketplace with property is initiated, then there is no logical (or pragmatic political) point at which to draw the line. The result would be to make the acquisition of property a social rather than an individual process, and that would subvert the entire philosophy — and practice — of capitalism.

It is of course true that the legacy of prejudice against the Negro, because of his inferior position in past times, reinforced this more general argument from the principles of the system. So, too, did the competitive agitation by special groups of Northern and Southern whites. But those factors operated within the framework of capitalism per se. As Wendell Phillips and a few other bourgeois socialists gradually realized, social treatment of the freed Negro implied social treatment of everyone else, and that implied a wholesale change in the very nature of the system.

Prejudice against the Negro therefore operated, and has continued to operate, as a factor limiting his freedom within the system.

It has restricted his ability to enter the marketplace. Even if that were overcome, however, the Negro would still find himself defined primarily in terms of his ego rather than in terms of a social being. The experience of the Negro jazz musician perfectly illustrates this point. His ordeal since the Civil War has revealed how overcoming prejudice to the point of being admitted to the marketplace because of especially marketable talents, skills, and labor does not serve to define the individual as a whole human being, or to produce acceptance and treatment of him in such broader terms. The labor he alienates to the marketplace is purchased and his social existence remains essentially unchanged. Admission to the marketplace should not be discounted, but its limitations should be understood. For the marketplace, as the rich as well as the poor white can verify, does not transform the ego into the soul.

The nineteenth-century assault by the Negro against prejudice, as revealed in the program of Booker T. Washington and his followers, was wholly conceived within the marketplace framework. In the beginning, moreover, Washington additionally limited the Negro's portion of the marketplace to that section involving "first-rate mechancial laborers." His educational program was designed to produce responsible, but essentially unskilled, workers for the lower end of the industrial system. In later years, it is true, he encouraged the Negro to become a businessman, but he retained the early bias against any true integration by emphasizing the need to be a Negro businessman hiring Negro workers.

Washington was actually recommending, though he may not have been wholly aware of it, that the Negro construct his own separate marketplace. This contradicted his avowed hope that business success would bring social acceptance by the white man. Some Negroes did become businessmen, but as E. Franklin Frazier has observed, that achievement was not very rewarding: "their lives generally lose both content and significance."

White bourgeois reformers were not noticeably more successful, even though they had a much larger marketplace in which to work. Despite their persistent efforts and their significant but limited victories, the men and women whom Marx referred to as bourgeois socialists were unable to overcome the central failure of the system by putting the two halves of man back together again within a capitalist framework. They did not, for an obvious example, seriously weaken prejudice against the Negro. For that matter, they assigned rather low priority to the task. Nor did they transform the white marketplace into a community. As these considerations suggest, bourgeois socialists were limited by the boundaries of their own ideas as well as by their opposition.

The reform movement also proved incapable of preventing the recurrence of grave economic depressions and severe social dislocations. Most ironic of all, perhaps, it did not prevent the very efficiency and productive capacity of the farmer as entrepreneur from driving the farmers as individuals into increasing difficulties or bankruptcy, and into a subordinate position in the system. If the farmer had been less successful as a producer, and thereby sustained his numbers, the mere fact of industrialization would not have created nearly so many troubles for him. His political power would not have been reduced to the extent that it was, and his social position would not have deteriorated so rapidly or extensively. In effect, the farmer was the first example of a large plurality of entrepreneurs reducing itself to a special interest group as a consequence of succeeding within the ground rules of capitalism.

As indicated by the case of the farmer, the reformers were generally unable to sustain the effective power of the individual property holder against either the giant entrepreneur or the rise of the joint-stock corporation. Both were the product of the competitive dynamic of the marketplace and represented a logical and natural result of the central axiom of capitalism that the individual had an inherent right to alienate his labor in the way that he considered most appropriate to his own interests.

Reformers offered three main proposals to preserve the role of the individual. Anti-trust legislation was designed to forestall monopoly. Combined with the sophisticated estimate of their own interests made by the emerging giants, which led them to support certain kinds of regulation so that they could control it, the anti-trust campaign was effective within that conceptual framework. But the real problem concerned the consolidation of an overweening oligarchy within each industry, and thereby in the system. Anti-trust legislation did not prevent that development.

A second, and related, reform drive attempted to guarantee equitable treatment to all entrepreneurs in the physical market-place, and involved extensive regulation or outright government ownership of the transportation and communications network. This was nationalization, true enough, but not in the socialist sense. The bourgeois socialists were concerned to nationalize the rudimentary circulatory system of the marketplace in order to preserve private property and capitalism in the fundamental sense. They were not so-cialists in any significant respect.

The reformers had more success in winning support for their third alternative, a renewed push to expand the American market-place through overseas economic expansion. To avoid any confusion on this point, it is worthwhile to re-emphasize that the reformers generally opposed acquiring formal colonies. This made them anti-colonial, but it did not make them anti-expansionist even in a general sense, and it most certainly did not lead them to oppose an American economic empire. They understood very clearly that a powerful national economy did not have to construct a formal colonial empire in order to expand its marketplace and control a sizeable share of the economic activity in the enlarged area.

Just as they were leaders in domestic reform, the farmers were also among the first to mount any sustained agitation for the expansion of the American marketplace under the aegis of the government. They manifested almost no interest in colonies, but they rapidly became supporters of a large modern navy with the necessary advance bases, of an isthmian canal controlled by the United States, and of a general policy of government action to open and protect new overseas markets. In their minds, moreover, their agitation for monetizing silver was inherently and irrevocably tied to their drive for more export markets. Trade and silver were for them two synonyms for talking about the same subject.

A vast number of urban businessmen, intellectuals, and politicians advocated the same policy. Some of them did so as reformers. Others interpreted the need for expansion from the point of view of their particular interest in the marketplace. And a small group of men thought within the framework of the kind of corporation capitalism that was beginning to reorganize the system created by the classic nineteenth-century entrepreneur. They understood that the change from the individual capitalist to the corporation would not alter the necessity of an ever-expanding marketplace. They anticipated that part of that need would be met by enlarging the home market, but they also argued that overseas operations would become increasingly important.

The real paradox in this situation does not concern the expansionism of the reformers—agrarian or urban. That perplexity disappears immediately once the reformers are recognized as the entrepreneurs they were. The paradox does not even involve the actual policy victory of the anti-colonial expansionists, even though the demise of their formal organization, the Anti-Imperialist League, suggests that they suffered a shattering defeat. After all, a good many successful critics become supporters of the new status quo they have helped create; and this was precisely what happened in the case of the Anti-Imperialists. They embraced the Open Door Policy and became firm supporters of that kind of overseas economic expansion.

The true paradox is that the reformers won the policy fight over the *kind* of expansion by stressing the vital importance – and even the sanctity – of the very marketplace forces that were then subverting the individual entrepreneur as the key element in the system. But the reformers of the nineteenth century had no other central axioms upon which to construct their own programs. They could hardly save capitalism by abandoning capitalism. Hence their very loyalty to the principles of the system destroyed their effective power to protect and preserve one particular form of the system.

They could not argue about anything except the *means* of expansion, because they could not deny the necessity of expansion without disavowing the basic premise of the system. And they impaled themselves upon the same forked spit in domestic affairs. The corporation triumphed and brought with it still another form of capitalist organization. But the principles of possessive individualism operating in a competitive marketplace remained the cornerstones of the system itself.

IV. EFFORTS TO TRANSCEND THE SYSTEM: "CORPORATION SOCIALISM"

*W*e are now a nation of wage and salaried employees and, in the main, we work for corporations.

Edward S. Mason,
*The Corporation in
Modern Society*

*N*or do I wish to be misinterpreted as believing that the United States is a free-for-all and devil-take-the-hindmost. The very essence of equality of opportunity and of American individualism is that there shall be no domination by any group or combination in this republic, whether it be business or political. On the contrary, it demands economic justice as well as political and social justice. It is no system of laissez faire.

Herbert Clark Hoover,
October 22, 1928

THE triumph of the corporation, and the creation of an oligarchy of firms within each sector of the economy, was a natural outcome of the principles of possessive individualism operating in a competitive marketplace. Such a marketplace has an ecology of its own, and that largely explains why businessmen found Darwinism such a useful ideology at the end of the nineteenth century. The analogy with nature is more helpful, however, if it is made on a less grandiose scale than that employed by the Social Darwinists. The ecological balance of the marketplace is predicated upon a coincidence between the interest and the need of the giants to accumulate capital and the desire of the defeated entrepreneurs to retain, and of the would-be businessman to attain, some measure of citizenship in the capitalist society. This convergence of interest and need produced what Marx called the modern joint-stock company, usually referred to as the corporation.

In recent years, largely as part of the propaganda battle with the Soviet Union, this broad process has been praised as People's Capitalism. The slogan has not generated much enthusiasm because most people realize that the average purchase of stock does not buy any significant share in the decision-making process of the system. Indeed, the campaign to sell the idea of People's Capitalism offers one of the more plaintive examples of the general failure of American capitalism to create a true community.

But it is true that capitalist principles operating in and through the corporation have served to impose a new and extensive rationality on the marketplace, and to boost the material output of the system far beyond anything previously attained. Marx himself seemed to stand in awe of what he called "the stupendous productive power" of corporation capitalism. Clearly enough, it has created — even without the final rationalization of cybernated production — the possibility of material affluence. The outpouring of goods and services is almost literally incomprehensible. Try to imagine, for example, a metaphor that will provide any meaningful image of the number of simple, old-fashioned wooden pencils manufactured in America in one year. Or bobby pins. Or bobby soxers full of anxiety for the latest edition of the magazines that offer reassurance by telling them how to spend the next allowance.

Since these examples derive from the use of science in the marketplace, they may also provide some insight into the process through which science attracts people by reducing difficult human problems into non-human terms. Science deals with one reality by creating another reality. It copes with the world of nature by inventing a universe of abstractions. We have so far maintained a precarious bridge between those two worlds through technology, which translates the scientific abstractions back into this-worldly objects. But that very technology may in the end re-define man himself as no more than a part of his products. This would reverse the humanistic tradition of seeing the products as the creation and projection of man. We would, in this sense, triumph over the alienation inherent in possessive individualism by becoming integrated with the things made by unattended machines.

That, of course, is precisely what Marx was worried about. And he understood that advanced capitalism was the form in which possessive individualism, operating through the competitive marketplace, might well alienate man from his humanity. Its power to provide affluence could also manufacture a new man, because in destroying individual property as a meaningful element in the marketplace it would subvert capitalistic man's basic definition of his own existence and leave him no sign or substance of his existence save the symbols provided by the material artifacts he possessed. He would participate in the system only as he stood at the end of the assembly line and collected commodities.

Marx did not live long enough to speak explicitly about the national class created by the corporation, or about corporation capitalism's own particular expression of the phenomenon he called feudal socialism and bourgeois socialism when it appeared in the earlier eras of capitalism. It is not particularly difficult, however, to make the appropriate extrapolation of his central ideas. Corporation capitalism has clearly produced such a national class in the persons of the large corporation's directors, administrators, experts, and an associated group of politicians and intellectuals.

This contemporary system is far closer, in both the structural sense and in the nature of its national class, to the capitalism created during the age of mercantilism than to the society of nineteenth-century entrepreneurial capitalism. These similarities offer, indeed, a helpful insight into the essential difficulties confronted by modern American capitalism. On the one hand, the productive power of the corporation offers the means whereby the secular part of the outlook of mercantilism might be translated into action. But, on the other hand, the functioning of capitalism since the era of mercantilism has severely weakened — if not effectively destroyed — the inclusive social and moral conception of society that was an integral part of mercantilism; and it has, in addition, produced so many changes in the non-Metropolitan areas of the world that it is impossible any longer to sustain the imperial aspects of mercantilism.

Contemporary American corporation capitalism is comparable to the mercantilist system, not only in the sense that stockholding of consequence is highly concentrated in a tiny fraction of the adult population, but also in the more significant respect that wealth and participation in the decision-making process of the entire political economy are likewise consolidated within a very small group. Although some of their superficial reactions might indicate otherwise, Americans do not suffer in ignorance of these truths that their society is structured by and around the corporation, or that its affairs are generally managed by a small and powerful community composed of the leaders of the economic, the political, and the military sectors of the system.

The lack of any sustained, excited public criticism and opposition to the existing situation, however, is based on the performance of the national class as well as upon the dearth of well-defined and vigorously advocated alternatives, and upon the great difficulty of changing the central features of the system. This national class has a defensible record, for example, if capitalism (or socialism, for that matter) is defined in a loose and general way as an institutional arrangement for providing increasing access to a greater range of material goods and services. And that is precisely the primary way that the principles of capitalism do define achievement. When the resulting pattern of production and consumer credit is furthermore linked, as it always is, with the successful defense of the nation in two wars and one cold war, the argument obscures the costs and consequences of the performance — and even many of the outright failures — with the emotion of nationalism. This chain of reasoning results in a superficially impressive balance account that camouflages the elementary truth: if capitalism did its narrow economic cost accounting in the same way it does its general social cost accounting, the system would have gone bankrupt within two generations.

It nevertheless remains true that the national class of corporation capitalism, particularly as it has been influenced by the reformers that Marx might have called the corporation socialists, has in some respects performed in keeping with the ideals and the tradition of responsibility associated with mercantilism. This became more noticeable after it began, at the time of World War I, to absorb and integrate many of its critics within its own community of power. It of course used force against such heretics as Eugene Debs whenever they seemed to be winning significant support for a challenge to the system. But the critics who operated within the limits of capitalism have gradually been accepted as participating advisors (and even subordinate administrators), or effectively weakened by using their ideas while ignoring their persons. Coupled with the pressure exerted by such critics, this strategy employed by the national class ultimately created a framework of regulatory and compensatory legislation that included ground rules for the corporation and various kinds of minimum (and still insufficient) support and assistance for the sizable number of citizens not taken care of by the normal functioning of the system.

Most of these administrative and welfare provisions emerged as a result of the Great Depression, and have been sustained as part of the response to the more general challenge to the system manifested by the social and colonial revolutions which erupted in full force at the end of World War II. But the process itself began during the era of President William McKinley, Marcus Hanna, and the National Civic Federation at the turn of the century.

McKinley and Hanna were conservatives who perceived the need to create and maintain a consensus including all segments of the new corporation order, and to offer all such elements a minimum share of the benefits of the new system. They understood that the corporation was so powerful that it would destroy the social fabric if it operated unchecked in the fashion of the giant entrepreneurs of the nineteenth century. They were not reformers, and they undoubtedly erred in the direction of preserving what to them seemed the essential freedom of the corporation. But they did hold and act on the basic features of the broader view that was essential to the creation of a national class.

The National Civic Federation was an indirect outgrowth of the early efforts by corporation socialists to reform the system. In its early stages, at any rate, it was a catholic organization which included such labor leaders as Samuel Gompers, and such aristocrats with a tradition of *noblesse oblige* as young Franklin Delano Roosevelt, as well as corporation executives. Though it played a significant role in establishing the idea and the existence of a national class, it ultimately became a narrowly conservative organization. As this happened, the more perceptive members of the national class itself, as well as the reformers, attempted to achieve their objectives by operating in and through the Progressive movement.

As a coalition including nineteenth-century bourgeois reformers and men who accepted the order created by the corporation, the Progressive movement fluctuated between trying to protect the traditional entrepreneur and endeavoring to rationalize and reform the new system. The early result of this divided effort was a hodgepodge of legislation. While in some respects appropriate to both objectives, it did not culminate in any single coherent pattern. Part of it flowed from the leadership provided by strong presidents like Theodore Roosevelt and Woodrow Wilson. Other laws emerged from the initiative manifested (and the compromises reached) within state legislatures and the Congress. And still other parts of this legislation, including some of the most important laws, represented the efforts of the leaders of the corporation's national class to check the more militant critics by accepting — and managing — some rational reforms.

Prior to the Great Depression, the creation of the Federal Reserve System was probably the single most important achievement of the coalition of the national class and the reformers. Further legislation of a comparable nature was passed during the New Deal era. While sometimes spoken of as a revolution, the New Deal was in reality the culmination of the Progressive movement and represented an operating consensus among the most astute members of the national corporation class and the reformers (or corporation socialists). It saved rather than changed the system, and thus can fairly be considered the finest performance of the national class and its associated reformers.

While it warrants high praise within its own framework and limits, this effort did not overcome the structural economic difficulties of the system, it did not initiate institutional and policy reforms that evolved into solutions of such problems, it did not revitalize the capitalist conception of citizenship and representative government, and it did not transform corporation capitalism into an ethical and equitable community. These failures had been anticipated, moreover, by a few members of the national class, as well as by critics who analyzed the situation from a vantage point outside the coalition of corporation spokesmen and reformers. The reformers concentrated their attention on the conservatives and the radicals, and hence did not contribute as much as they might have to raising and answering the fundamental questions.

One of the most striking evaluations of the weaknesses of the system was offered during the 1920's by Herbert Clark Hoover. This facet of Hoover's performance as a member of the national class is usually overlooked, and he is seldom thought of as a social commentator along with such figures as Brooks Adams, Herbert Croly, or Walter Lippmann. The neglect is understandable in view of his far more active career as an economic and government leader, and his ill-deserved reputation as both the cause of the Great Depression and as the man who failed to stop it immediately. But the negligence obscures his several important insights into the failure of corporation capitalism to create a true community.

Hoover not only understood the nature of the problems which confronted the national class, but astutely recognized the dangers involved in the new corporation order. Provoked by his concern that no incisive, sustained effort was being made to control the inherent propensities of the system, he projected three possible avenues of devolution. If left to themselves to provide the membership and the policies of the national class, Hoover feared that the corporation leaders would produce an American form of fascism. If labor became predominant, on the other hand, the result would be socialism or some willy-nilly variation thereof that would be equally undesirable. If each broad interest group in the economy continued its evolving attitude of viewing the government as a marketplace in which to compete for its share of the gross wealth, then the system would ultimately be dominated by a state bureaucracy which would lack even the distinguishing characteristic of a positive ideology. And wars engendered by struggles for predominance in the world marketplace threatened to produce a tyranny of even graver proportions because of the increased role and influence of the military.

Wherever it came from, perhaps his Quaker family background and his education at Stanford, Hoover enjoyed a clear insight into the crucial importance of reinvigorating and strengthening the social, co-operative half of man if capitalism was to survive economically and create a true community. He did not propose to destroy the traditional capitalist definition of the ego in terms of possessive individualism in the competitive marketplace, but he did want to delimit and balance it by reasserting the social definition of man as an ethical, co-operative being. He thus proposed, as he tried to explain in a misleadingly titled and generally misread essay called *American Individualism*, that American capitalism should cope with its economic problems by voluntaristic but nevertheless organized co-operation within and between each major sector of the economy. This would in turn revitalize social life and representative government.

As he made explicitly clear as early as 1919, Hoover was consciously trying to balance "the immutable human qualities" of "selfishness" and "altruism" through the use of man's will power and intelligence, and through a broad program of education. He faced the issue posed by the capitalist marketplace more directly than most of his contemporaries — or successors. If the system could not be made to work through self-control and "by cooperation," Hoover concluded at the end of World War I, then it would be "better that we accept German domination and confess the failure of our political ideas, acquiesce in the superiority of the German conception and send for the Germans to instruct us in its use." Having arrived at this estimate of the alternatives, Hoover committed himself to the proposition that the co-operative ideal could be realized in practice.

Hoover's failure to accomplish this gargantuan task was due less to the depression per se, or even to his own inability to act because of his deep-seated fears of driving the system into one of the cul-de-sacs he had spotted in advance, than to the inherent nature of the undertaking itself. Despite the austere nature of his style and personality, which seem to belie the very idea, Hoover was actually proposing to socialize capitalism without socializing the economic system. Whether this was really a contradiction in terms, and therefore an unrealizable vision, can be left a moot question; it is enough to point out that it would have been a Herculean task under the very best of circumstances. It was in effect an attempt to do under corporation capitalism what the mercantilists such as John Quincy Adams had tried, and ultimately failed, to do in the seventeenth and eighteenth centuries.

Unfortunately, neither Hoover nor others who shared the same general objective have been able to realize the goal. But a good many of the attempts to accomplish it, which are usually associated with President Franklin Delano Roosevelt and the New Deal (and subsequent variations thereon), have been derived from Hoover's own efforts. One of these, which has lately returned to favor, involves his persistent campaign to persuade American farmers to establish themselves as the equals of the industrial corporation (and the labor unions) by organizing co-operatives through which they could control their production and manage their marketing operations.

Another illustration of Hoover's foresight is offered by his militant opposition in the 1920's to turning the atmosphere, which he considered social property in the most elementary sense, over to the corporations as an arena in which they could stage a free-for-all over profits to the suffering of the citizen radio (and later television) listener. Hoover instituted strong restrictions on the radio industry while he was Secretary of Commerce; so strong, indeed, that they were overruled by the Attorney General after sustained protests from the corporations. The law substituted by the Congress was considerably less effective. But however weak and ineffective they have been in limiting the abuses of the industry, or in improving the quality of its product, the Federal Radio Commission and the later Federal Communications Commission owe their existence to Hoover's original willingness to act upon a broad conception of social responsibility. Similar actions initiated by Hoover, including the effort to establish good neighbor relations with Latin America, were expanded by later administrations which received most, if not all, of the credit for whatever successes they produced.

Hoover's most pertinent and trenchant criticism has been generally ignored by members of the national class, and even more noticeably by the reformers. The reason for this is that both groups have attempted to sustain the system by following the precise course of action that Hoover judged most severely as being inequitable and ultimately unsuccessful. This strategy of saving the system was initiated by some industrialists and reformers before World War I, and then agitated militantly by the farm bloc in the 1920's. Its central theme was that the government should give direct and indirect subsidies to sustain various functional groups of entrepreneurs in the marketplace, such funds to be provided by the taxpayers present and future.

Hoover assailed and fought such proposals on several grounds. They subjected the citizen to double payments for goods and services, since in addition to the price paid over the counter, the consumer-taxpayer contributed to the same firms through the internal revenue service. Such subsidies also opened the door to, and actually legalized, wholesale raids on the federal treasury — meaning the pocketbook of the public. And they would, at least in Hoover's mind, lead to the kind of bureaucratic state capitalism that he considered so dangerous because it pointed toward fascism or some variation thereof. Hoover insisted that saving capitalism by juggling subsidies drawn from the taxpayer would ultimately "lead to the destruction of self-government," because as the government became so intimately involved in the system the citizen would lose his ability to act independently. His own self-interest would become so intimately bound to the government-corporation complex that the alternatives he was offered would concern only means rather than ends.

Hoover's analysis and warnings were lost or discounted as the subsidy approach was adopted and institutionalized during the crisis of the depression. It may have been impossible for corporation capitalism to have sustained itself in any other fashion, but the results nevertheless make it necessary to evaluate the system's material achievements in the light of its general inability to create an ethical and equitable community. *This failure evolved from the decision to shore up the corporation political economy by using the government to accumulate social capital from the taxpayer. This capital was then used to maintain the existing pattern of private control over the system. The government thus adapted the corporation's technique of accumulating capital from individual entrepreneurs without offer-*

ing or providing such investors any significant share in making basic decisions. Instead of socializing the system without socializing property, the result was to socialize the accumulation of capital without socializing control of the capital.

Confronted with the threatened demise of the system itself in the Great Depression, the coalition of the national class and the reformers undertook to save and rationalize the existing order through a further expansion of the marketplace and a vastly enlarged collection and use of taxes. The United States became a tax state in the fullest sense: the rules for collecting the funds, and the budget by which they were allocated, became in effect the X-ray photographs of the structure of the system and the priorities by which it operated.

In thus socializing the accumulation of capital, however, the New Deal did not socialize either the decisions concerning the allocation of that capital or the distribution of wealth in the United States. Even moderately heavy taxation of the upper class, for example, did not come during the reform period of the New Deal, but only as the nation prepared to enter World War II. And as that action was undertaken, moreover, the New Deal also extended the income tax to the middle and lower income classes on a retrogressive basis. The national class clearly had vastly more to say about the allocation of these funds than the citizens who paid them; and, since the funds had by definition to be used primarily for sustaining the key productive elements in the established order, the industrial corporation, the giant agricultural units, and other large operators received fantastically greater returns on their investment in taxes than the individual or small entrepreneur.

This expansion of the tax base occurred between 1939, when four million units were liable to pay, through 1941, when 17.6 million were obligated, to 1944, when the number so bound reached 42.4 million. The retrogressive nature of the resulting system is revealed in many ways. The tax paid in 1957 by the average family in the poorest fifth of the population, which was 3.3 percent, for example, was clearly a greater burden than the 13.7 percent paid by the average family in the richest fifth of the society. The tax ratio between poor and wealthy was 1:4, whereas the income ratio was approximately 1:11.

Another indication of the nature of the system is provided by comparing the taxes collected from Americans who earn between $1 and $4,000 with the amount spent by the federal government on welfare programs. The sum collected from the poor during 1958 was $6.037 billion. The government spent a total of $4.509 billion on all its public assistance programs, its public health operations, its aid to education, and all other welfare programs. That sum includes, furthermore, half the cost of farm supports and half the total spent on housing programs. It is thus apparent that the poorest people are not only paying their own way on welfare, but are providing part of the public assistance for the middle- and upper-class citizens.

The high income groups are of course entitled to those benefits. The issue here is how the tax system instituted by the New Deal and sustained by later reform administrations is skewed to favor the higher income groups. This can be seen even more directly from figures for the top 20 percent of the income earners. They received 45.7 percent of all personal income before taxes in 1959, and still had 43.8 percent of it after taxes. And when the vast sums deducted from gross incomes as business expenses, including entertainment as well as depreciation, are considered, the imbalance becomes even greater and more obvious. In the central area of tax collection and allocation, therefore, corporation capitalism has failed even to approximate an ethical and equitable system.

It has done little better in dealing with the problem of poverty. There is no conceivable ethical justification, or support in equity, for either the kind or the extent of poverty that exists today in the United States. It is a blot not only upon American society per se, but a standing monument to the inability of corporation capitalism to include everyone in its economic benefits, even though everyone contributes through taxes (and even voluntary welfare and medical gifts) to its operating capital. It is a system and a government which has *by its actions* given a higher priority to putting machines into space than to sustaining life within its own boundaries.

Even as subsidized, moreover, corporation capitalism has failed to sustain a viable economy. Significant and persistent unemployment continues, and many existing jobs will be destroyed or downgraded (and thereby dehumanized) if cybernation continues within the existing framework. The programs to cope with these current difficulties —let alone the problems clearly on the horizon—are inadequate in conception and insufficient in extent. The same judgment is warranted in connection with slum clearance (which has notoriously benefited the middle class and the wealthy rather than the poor), with metropolitan and continental transportation, with care of the sick and invalided, with programs for the young and aged alike, and with education in general.

Perhaps this failure of corporation capitalism to meet either the narrow economic or the broader social needs and challenges of contemporary America is most aptly typified in the almost obsessive concern with the growth rate of the system. Now the economy obviously has to grow if only to keep pace with population increases. But this definition of the problem is not really to the point, anymore than a discussion of the growth rate in terms of the current or projected Russian figure confronts the real issue. For the *existing* capacity of the established order is capable of producing enough to relegate the contemporary growth discussion to a secondary level. The real problems concern how to use that capacity, and how to initiate and sustain a dialogue about the further growth of what, for what, at what cost, and decided by whom through what process. Yet there is almost no candid debate about those matters which lie at the very heart of creating an ethical and equitable community.

By defining any and all changes needed to meet these and similar issues as being dangerous to the existing order, the leaders of the system are forced to make such alterations behind the scenes, if they make them at all. This extends the already extensive centralization of power within the national class and within the government per se. The result may well be the disappearance of the existing pattern of private control over social production and its replacement by a system of administrative control over bureaucratic production. This would most certainly not be socialism. It would not even be fascism, at least not of the kind evolved in Italy and Germany during the 1920's and 1930's. It would be a kind of eerie and distorted verification of Herbert Hoover's fear that the government in becoming the marketplace would also become the corporation to end all corporations. It would be a corporation, furthermore, controlled by inside administrators only fitfully checked or directed by the citizen through the political process.

All this serves to dramatize the extent to which representative government has already broken down under corporation capitalism. The logic of possessive individualism operating in a competitive marketplace is presently creating a system in which neither the entrepreneur nor the wage earner has a fulcrum upon which to rest his political lever. Political units no longer coincide even roughly with economic and social reality. Issues are of necessity cast, and men elected, within a framework that has a steadily *decreasing* relevance to the nature of problems, simply because the existing political ground rules require a multiple distortion of the issues in order to piece together the required number of electoral votes to win access to the top executive and administrative offices.

Though it presents a very serious problem that will not be solved simply through continued urbanization and industrialization, the issue of political organization per se is actually secondary. The heart of the problem lies in the question facing both major parties concerning the formulation of relevant alternatives within the limits of capitalist ideology. The corporation, as Marx pointed out, represents "private production without the control of private property." The stockholders do not formulate or choose between alternatives. Neither do the labor unions. And most certainly the taxpaying citizens do not. Marx was essentially correct: the corporation itself, and the political economy it dominates, rests upon the "command of social capital" through the "appropriation of social property" by the small decision-making community which makes up the national class of the system.

In theory, at any rate, this leadership community could involve the citizen in the decisions affecting the allocation of the social capital. In order to do so, however, the decision-makers would first have to admit candidly that the system operates on the basis of the appropriation of social capital from the taxpayer as well as from the individual investor. Then the national class would have to formulate its internal differences into competing programs and policies, and reorganize the political system around such groups. Then the citizen would have an opportunity to choose between the rival segments of the national class. This would be an improvement over the existing situation, to be sure, but it would still represent a very low order of representative government. For the citizen who supplies the capital would still be denied any significant part in formulating the choices.

Even this first step in rationalizing the existing system would require an open admission that the reality of the system has little if any relationship to the ideology of the system. It would involve an acknowledgement that private property no longer provides the individual with any significant leverage upon the central decisions of the political economy. And to say that is to say that the individual no longer attains freedom through exercising his right to alienate part of himself as labor in a competitive marketplace. For the property he thereby acquires does not affect the marketplace, either directly or indirectly.

The principles of capitalism have produced a reality in which the principles no longer hold true. Man does not become human and free by acting within the axioms of possessive individualism and the competitive marketplace. Instead, he becomes alienated. He is free to choose only among alternatives, and on issues, which no longer effect the nature of the society. He is becoming a mere consumer of politics as well as a mere consumer of goods. The sharing of profits is mistaken for the sharing of direction and control of the enterprise itself, just as the sharing of the leader's charisma is mistaken for the sharing of power.

This process is the negative side of what Marx had in mind when he spoke of the "socialization from within" brought on by the corporation. The corporation has socialized the accumulation of capital: directly through the substitution of money rights for property (or control) rights, and indirectly by effecting a liaison through its national class with the government of the tax state. The system relies on social accumulation but tries to operate on the classical capitalist principle of private control. It is unable on this basis either to sustain efficient economic operation or to create an ethical and equitable community.

Perhaps capitalism can rest content with this by no means inconsiderable achievement of having demonstrated beyond a reasonable doubt that neither man nor freedom can be defined as the acquisitive ego. To have done that, after all, is to have cleared the way, and to have provided the material base, for an inconceivably free, human, and creative future. If such a future also involves and requires a broader definition of man and freedom than capitalism is based upon, the capitalist can hardly blame the critic for that state of affairs. It has been the capitalist operating on capitalist principles, after all, who has demonstrated the limitations of capitalism. All the critic is doing is judging the system as created and sustained by its own proponents, and concluding that its acknowledged achievements and benefits include a demonstration that man cannot be defined in terms of his possessions. Marx was absolutely correct in his argument of a century ago that man does not live by production and commodities alone.

T*he Central Utility of Marx*

The call to abandon [our] illusions about [our] condition is a call to abandon a condition which requires illusions.

Karl Marx, 1843

Finally, let us consider, by way of change, a community. . . .

Karl Marx, 1867

The philosophers have only *interpreted* the world in different ways; the point is to *change* it.

Karl Marx, 1845

*T*HE central utility of Karl Marx for Americans in the middle of the twentieth century is that he is a heretic who helps us by bringing our capitalistic ego into a confrontation with our capitalist reality. As with the groom and the horse, the philosopher can lead us to the self-examination, but he cannot make us change our ways. Only we can do that. But there is no doubt as to the value of the philosopher—however we cope with his challenge.

When examined seriously and soberly, the evidence submitted by American capitalism fails to confirm either the popular stereotype or the official myth about Karl Marx. The United States has not proved that Marx was wrong. The overall achievement of American capitalism, even with the peacetime subsidies provided by the non-entrepreneurial taxpayer, and with the further direct and indirect assistance flowing from wars and cold wars, can at most be characterized as a high-level stalemate with the internal forces that Marx identified as driving capitalism toward breakdown under normal circumstances. And, in cybernated production, American capitalism would seem to have fulfilled its axioms and logic in a way that Marx saw as providing both the basis and the reason for a transition to a new order of political economy.

In its non-economic aspects, moreover, which Marx properly insisted were an integral part of the system per se, American capitalism offers countless examples, at both the individual and the group levels, of the harmful and dangerous devolutions that he feared and anticipated. The economic achievement has been purchased at very great costs in human and material resources. The Negro is still not integrated even into the marketplace, let alone the society, a full century after capitalism destroyed the neo-feudal Southern society based on slavery. And possessive individualism operating in a competitive marketplace has increasingly proletarianized and stratified American society.

The individual displays increasing signs, overt and unconscious, of alienation, disorientation, and anti-social behavior. The integrated personality, let alone the integrated group, is produced only in opposition to the status quo, rather than by and through a commitment to the avowed principles of the system. Perhaps the most disturbing evidence of all concerns the way Americans have denied the very conception and idea of Utopia in the name of practicality, pragmatism, and realism. The metaphor of space, which was once a symbol of William Blake's cosmos that awaited man's fertile and creative and transcending genius, has been transformed into a literal area in which to repeat the old frontier habit of conquering a new and virgin territory and then making it over in the image of the old society.

In the realm of foreign affairs, meanwhile, Marx's analysis and predictions have withstood the test of changing reality in an even more dramatic way. From the seventeenth century to the present, the capitalist commitment to expanding the marketplace has guided and set limits upon American foreign policy. It defined relationships with Africa and the Negro, with the North American continent and the Indian (and even among the whites for control of the continent), and with the underdeveloped societies and nations (and, through them, with other industrial countries).

In each of these cases—the Negro, the Indian, the South, and the underdeveloped areas—the expansion of the American marketplace brought grave and painful consequences to the non-Metropolitan elements. After having been forcibly transferred from his home as a chattel colonial, the Negro was belatedly released from that condition only to be defined and treated as an unequal and hence unfree ego in the marketplace. The Indians who survived suffered a similar fate. The South is even today a depressed, backward, and unequal sector of the Metropolis. And the inherent inequality in the marketplace relationship between the Metropolis and the underdeveloped countries has led, as Marx forecast that it would, to increasing misery for the poor nations and to a determination on their part to break free of that inequitable imperial relationship.

Despite the flood of material artifacts constantly spewed forth by modern capitalism, therefore, these far more significant failures have produced an intellectual and moral malaise which confronts American capitalism with grave difficulties as it faces the clear and present need to initiate a graceful, generous, and dignified — *and effective* — transition to a post-capitalist order. This weariness has the effect of limiting even the most intelligent and concerned leaders to a range of choices which does not reach to the heart of the crisis. They propose and consider alternatives which, even at their best, never break through the conception of reforming and thereby saving the established system.

Such reform might be possible, at least for a time. The power and the momentum of the existing system will no doubt sustain it for a certain interval even without drastic reforms, and modifications of that nature might prolong its life for a significant period. This is not as certain, however, as the reformers hope and assert. The malfunctioning of the economic and political sectors is so serious and fundamental as to raise grave doubts about the viability of even an extensive repair job. And the social situaton is so critical that it may, in and of itself, prevent such reforms from being instituted. Even if this is not the case, the proposed changes do not promise any creative transcendence of the present condition.

This unsettling truth is, of course, the most devastating commentary on the strategy of reforming and saving the system. It offers nothing to inspire a commitment to the effort. Hence it is imperative to confront the true nature and the full scope of the crisis and break sharply and finally with the strategy of preservation.

The crisis created by cybernated production is THE *crisis of capitalism as defined by Marx. The capitalist system has in cyber-nated production fulfilled its promise and potential, and has created the absolute necessity to transcend its inability to cope with its own success. But capitalist leadership literally does not know—it cannot conceive—what to do at this magnificent turning point in human history that was so accurately foreseen by Karl Marx. If left to its limited devices and cramped imaginations, the turn will not be made.*

This essential change of course can only be made by following Marx's insights and morality, and thereby undertaking the creation of a true human community. Instead of residing in defining Marx as an enemy or as a problem, wisdom lies in grasping the Marxist critique firmly so that it can be used as a fulcrum with which to move both America and the world. This makes it possible, first of all, to admit the finite nature of capitalism without denying either its achievements or its role as the creator of conditions and means for something better. It offers, secondly, the positive challenge of creating a better society rather than the negative task of prolonging an existing system that is increasingly caught up in its own difficulties and limitations. And it presents, in the third place, a meaningful guide for meeting that challenge.

Marx is, after all, the paradoxical prophet of affluence and of the irrelevance of affluence once it is attained. "The realm of freedom does not commence," he pointed out, "until the point is passed where labor under the compulsion of necessity and of external utility is required. In the very nature of things it lies beyond the sphere of material production in the strict meaning of the term." Capitalism has created in cybernated production the tool to provide such affluence, but it cannot employ that tool to build a truly free community.

For, grounded as it is in the principle and the practice of possessive individualism, capitalism cannot break free of the conceptions and the institutions that define society as a marketplace system, and work as the process of alienating part of oneself in order to satisfy another part of oneself. Marx revitalizes, and offers for our consideration, the far more appropriate and classical conception of man as a social being, rather than as a competitive and alienated protagonist in the marketplace. "Only in association with others," Marx correctly insists, "has each individual the means of cultivating his talents in all directions. Only in a community therefore is personal freedom possible."

When Marx says that labor should cease to be "merely a means of life" and become instead "life's principle need," he is courageously substituting the classical meaning of work for the capitalist definition of man as a quantum of energy in the marketplace. He is saying that the central need of the individual is to fulfill himself in creative labor which produces relationships which humanize and strengthen and sustain his community with other individuals.

Marx did not define post-capitalist society — socialism and communism — as enlightened self-interest in a condition of glutinous satiation. He was not primarily concerned with how much man possessed. He assumed that the problems of meeting material needs and providing a diversity of goods were quite capable of being solved — even that they would be solved in the technical sense during the last phases of capitalism itself. Marx was concerned with the way man defined himself and his relationships with other men, and how he used his creativity once his basic needs had been satisfied.

Instead of being derived from Hobbes, Locke, and Smith, therefore, Marx's outlook was grounded in the classical tradition.* Ele-

*This discussion is indebted to John Anderson's series of articles in the *Australasian Journal of Psychology and Philosophy*. They began in 1927 and continue to the present. Eugene Kamenka provides a good introduction to the issues in *The Ethical Foundations of Marxism* (London: Routledge and Kegan Paul, 1962), especially pages 99 – 104; but the serious student should go on to Anderson's work.

ments of his thought can be traced back to Plato (as with Socrates in *Republic I,* and Glaucon in *Republic II*), to Aristotle, and to the Bible. The examples he repeatedly invoked were "the old Athens," the early Christians, and medieval feudal society. Marx's resulting *Weltanschauung* can be outlined in the following manner.

First. Man is a social as well as an egoistic being. Freedom is therefore defined as the reconciliation of the ego with the social, rather than by the unlimited exercise of the ego.

Second. The ego separates man from man. It makes him an exception to, rather than a member of, the human community.

Third. The objective is thus to end this separation between the egoistic interest and the common interest—or the community. This can only be done within the framework of the injunction to "love thy neighbor as thyself"; that is, by realizing that a man divided against another man is a man divided against himself. "Every man represents the other," Marx explained, "not through something else, which he symbolizes, but through that which he *is* and *does*." Individual dignity is thus defined by a situation "where we create independently within our own circle."

Marx's repeated references to feudal society have to be understood within this context. He saw feudalism as an order in which the egoistic and the social were linked through the relationships between people. To be sure, he idealized feudalism to some extent, but he did so knowingly, in an effort to provide a concrete example of the way in which the private and the public should be integrated. Whatever its failures, Marx explained, feudalism did involve a definition of *particular* interests and relationships in terms of *general* interests and relationships. The individual's "private, particular activity and situation" was part of "a general activity and situation."

His own formulation transcended feudalism. "Human emancipation will be complete only when the actual existing individual man takes back into himself the abstract citizen, when, as individual man, he has become a generic social being in his everyday life, in his individual work and in his individual relations." When, in short, he defines himself in terms of, and acts on, the injunction to love thy neighbor as thyself.

Fourth. In the specific moral sense, Marx bases his *Weltanschauung* upon the classical and Old Testament distinction between good and evil. A *good* is internally coherent; it can work with all objects and be extended indefinitely. An *evil*, on the other hand, is internally incoherent and unstable. It conflicts not only with a *good*, but with itself. It is thus repressive and destructive. A *good* co-operates and creates a harmonious whole. An *evil* produces atomistic separation and, ultimately, destructiveness.

Fifth. Freedom, therefore, is neither the definition and the exercise of the ego in terms of possessive individualism in the marketplace, nor simply an illusion. Free love, for example, is not the uninhibited sexual conquest of a multiplicity of objects. It is love free in the far more fundamental sense that it does not rely on illusions or restraints (sexual and otherwise) to exist. It is the voluntary and unhedged acknowledgment, transcending the mere sexual, of interdependence. Free thought is that which explores the dynamism of its assumptions without subordinating itself to one particular interim set of conclusions in order to protect particular interests or authorities. And a free society is that in which the individual defines himself, and acts, as a citizen of a community rather than as a competing ego. In a very real sense, therefore, the frontier for Marx is the space and resources made available for human development by loving thy neighbor as thyself.

Cybernated production has created the material base upon which we can stand to accept and take up the challenge to act upon this definition and vision of community. The effort will not be easy. It is no commitment for those whose idea of Utopia is early retirement on higher social security payments. But it is not impossible, and the interrelated aspects of the process can be outlined with enough clarity to reveal the broad kinds of action we will have to undertake, and to define the dialogue through which we will guide our continuing efforts.

We must begin by ceasing to limit our conception of humanity and freedom by tying it to the possession of property. Property is the night-light of the frightened and the banister for the immature. We must abandon this crutch of identity and learn to walk on our own. The point is not that we must abandon our possessions, but rather that we must re-define the possessions as incidental to our functioning as humans, instead of as crucial to our existence as humans. Once we recognize how little our property actually defines us today (or what a meager definition it provides), and how cybernated production can reduce property to an incidental if we use it to do so, this crisis of definition can be surmounted.

Hence the basic policy decision must be to undertake the planned, controlled, and co-ordinated movement into full cybernated production.

As we do this, we must initiate an open and sustained dialogue concerning the problems of creating and maintaining a balance between the non-economic and the economic, as well as among the economic, consequences of such a move into full cybernation. In and of itself, that is to say, the cybernation of the economy offers no insurmountable problems, but the real issues involve deciding what kind of a society we want when that has been done, and preparing ourselves for that moment of achievement. For unless we are prepared to act as true humans when we achieve full cybernation, we will be unable to cope with the psychological challenge of having either an identity or a creative purpose outside of the traditional capitalist one of work in the competitive marketplace.

This suggests that we must very carefully co-ordinate the full cybernation of the economy with a restructuring of the existing political system, and with a vast and intense educational program. The central guideline for all of this is provided by two central truths. First, a true community is more easily obtainable, and more extensively developed, in small rather than in large units. Second, cybernated production makes it possible to honor this axiom about community and at the same time meet economic needs and desires.

Hence the issue is not whether to decentralize the economy and the politics of the country, but rather how to do so. The solution here revolves about the regional elements that make up the existing whole. These must be defined, and then established as economic and political units grounded in their own co-operatively owned and controlled cybernated productive systems. The existing states need not be destroyed, for they can continue to function as units within the new regional elements. It is conceivable, however, that the citizens of some states would decide, for economic and other reasons, to divide in order to join different regional communities. This should of course be permitted.

In and of itself, this process will open up a tremendous arena for intellectual and political action across the next decade. The exhilarating experience of constitution-making will be carried on within and between a minimum of eight to ten new communities. In addition, and concurrently, each new regional and cybernated economy will have to be constructed, and its interrelationships defined and established. In order to do these things, furthermore, the educational system will have to be simultaneously reoriented and extended to provide the leadership required.

This literal restructuring and rebuilding of American society offers the only physical and intellectual challenge capable of absorbing and giving focus to the physical and intellectual resources of the country during the next generation. Indeed, a planned move into cybernated production within this framework will still leave sufficient resources to provide vastly increased aid and assistance to the underdeveloped nations, and to continue the rational (as opposed to the political) exploration of space.

Throughout such a process, moreover, the participants will be educating themselves—formally and informally, and without restrictions as to age—for their membership in the truly human community they will be creating. In the end they will have built a physical America which will be beautiful instead of ugly, and which will facilitate human relationships instead of dividing men into separate functional elements. They will have evolved a political system which is democratic in form and social in content. And they will be prepared, as cybernated production is completed, to function as men and women who can define their own identity, and their relationships with each other, outside the confining limits of property and the bruising and destructive dynamics of the competitive marketplace. They will be ready to explore the frontier of their own humanity.

It matters very little whether one calls this socialism or civilization. The issue is what kind of people we want to be and what kind of a world we want to have. Hence the question is whether or not we have the will, and the integrity, to admit that Marx was right in insisting that these are the central problems, and also right in saying that human rather than marketplace answers are the only objectives worthy of our commitment and our energy. If we meet that test, then we can get on with the task of transcending Marx's prophecy by creating an American community that will be beyond even his noblest dreams.

ACKNOWLEDGMENT

▾

I am grateful for two kinds of help which contributed to this book.

The Research Committee of the University of Wisconsin and the Louis Rabinowitz Foundation have given me indirect but significant financial assistance. Neither organization extended grants for this specific project, but a study of this nature draws on research done over a long period of time on a wide range of subjects. Both organizations have helped me defray the costs of such investigations.

I am likewise indebted, over many years, to my wholly friendly if occasionally heated conversations with William B. Hesseltine, Paul Farmer, Harvey Goldberg, Warren Susman, George Mosse, Hans Gerth, Lloyd Gardner, Omar Kussow, and Karl Paul Link; and to specific suggestions by Ivan Dee.

I also benefited from the information and ideas advanced by the students who participated in a seminar on Marx in Europe and America, held at the University of Wisconsin during the winter and spring of 1964 under the joint direction of George Mosse and myself.

I thank them all with warm affection and great respect.

A NOTE
ON STATISTICS

THE statistical data in the book is drawn primarily from various United States government publications and from the reports issued by international agencies. This literature is so vast as to proscribe full citation in an essay of this nature, particularly as any given figure may be the result of several calculations.

But, as examples of international reports, consult the publications of the United Nations Economic Commission for Latin America; David A. Morse, *Report of the Director General: Economic Growth and Social Policy. 7th Conference of American States Members of the International Labor Organization* (Geneva: International Labor Office, 1961); and the annual reports of the Inter-American Development Bank.

United States official documents include the myriad reports of the Bureau of the Census; the outpouring from the Departments of Labor and Commerce, typified by the *Monthly Labor Review* and the monthly *Survey of Current Business*; and such hearings as: U.S. Senate, Sub-Committee on Employment and Manpower of the Committee on Labor and Public Welfare, *Nation's Manpower Revolution* (Washington: U.S. Government Printing Office, 1963); and U.S. Congress, Joint Economic Committee, *Hearings on the 1963 Economic Report of the President* (Washington: U.S. Government Printing Office, 1963).

The analysis and interpretation of this data is almost as voluminous as the evidence itself. But see, as representative, the following items. The reader will find a good many disagreements over specific figures, but the main burden of the data is unmistakable. The significant differences concern what to do about the established condition. Michael Harrington, *The Other America: Poverty in the United States* (New York: Macmillan, 1962); Leon H. Keyserling, *Poverty and Deprivation in the U.S. — The Plight of Two-Fifths of a Nation* (Washington: Conference on Economic Progress, 1962); Gabriel Kolko, *Wealth and Power in America; An Analysis of Social Class and Income Distribution* (New York: Frederick A. Praeger, 1962); Edgar May, *The Wasted Americans: Cost of Our Welfare Dilemma* (New York: Harper and Row, 1964); Herman P. Miller, *Rich Man, Poor Man* (New York: Thomas Y. Crowell, 1964); Gunnar Myrdal, *Challenge to Affluence* (New York: Pantheon Books, 1963); Bernard D. Nossiter, *The Mythmakers: An Essay on Power and Wealth* (Cambridge: Houghton Mifflin Co., 1964); and Robert Theobald, *Free Men and Free Markets* (New York: Clarkson N. Potter, 1963).

▼

THE AUTHOR

William Appleman Williams was born in Atlantic, Iowa, in 1921. A graduate of the United States Naval Academy and a veteran of the war in the Pacific, he received his doctorate from the University of Wisconsin in 1950. He has taught at Washington and Jefferson, Bard College, Ohio State University, the University of Oregon and the University of Wisconsin, Madison. He is now Professor of History at Oregon State University. He has written extensively in historical journals and magazines of opinion and is the author of major works in history including *The Tragedy of American Diplomacy* (1959), and *The Contours of American History* (1961). Both have been translated in foreign countries and have forced a reassessment of many key issues in American history. Mr. Williams is thought by many to be one of the most influential historians writing in America today. His most recent work is *History as a Way of Learning,* published by New Viewpoints.